The Complete Ethical Landlord

Jack Donahue

Published by Defenestration Press, 2024.

While every precaution has been taken in the preparation of this book, the publisher assumes no responsibility for errors or omissions, or for damages resulting from the use of the information contained herein.

THE COMPLETE ETHICAL LANDLORD

First edition. May 14, 2024.

Copyright © 2024 Jack Donahue.

ISBN: 979-8224222377

Written by Jack Donahue.

Table of Contents

Introduction

Have you ever wondered what it takes to be an ethical landlord in a time when landlords are despised? In a world where the housing crisis is making headlines and tenants' rights protests are breaking out in every corner of the globe, it seems that being a landlord has become synonymous with greed, exploitation, and heartlessness. But is this really the case? Can there be such a thing as a compassionate, fair, and ethical landlord?

In my years of research and experience in the field, I have encountered countless tales of landlord horror stories. Tenants forced out of their homes, exorbitant rent increases, neglectful maintenance, and the constant fear of eviction. It is true that these stories exist, and they shed light on the dire need for change in the rental market. But let me ask you this, dear reader, does it have to be this way? Can landlords not also be champions of social responsibility, agents of positive change, and guardians of their communities?

Throughout this book, we will dig into the complex dynamics of the landlord-tenant relationship. We will examine the real-life challenges faced by both parties and reveal strategies for fostering empathy, fairness, and open communication. But before we begin, let me make one thing clear: being an ethical landlord does not mean sacrificing your own financial stability or neglecting your own needs. On the contrary, it is about finding a balance, creating a win-win situation where both landlord and tenant can thrive.

The Complete Ethical Landlord goes beyond theoretical concepts. It offers practical, actionable advice that you can implement right away. Whether you own a single unit or manage a vast portfolio of properties, this book is your roadmap to success. You will learn how to select tenants who align with your ethical values, how to develop and enforce clear policies that promote fairness and transparency, and how to maintain your properties in a manner that enhances the well-being of your tenants and the community at large.

But this book is not only for landlords. It is also for tenants who want to understand the other side of the equation and advocate for their own rights and well-being. By gaining insights into the mindset and responsibilities of ethical landlords, you will be better equipped to navigate the rental market and forge positive, harmonious relationships with your landlords.

As we embark on this journey, we must acknowledge the global housing crisis and its impact on society. The responsibility to address this crisis does not rest solely on the shoulders of landlords, but as key stakeholders in the housing market, we have the power to make a difference. By adopting ethical practices, we can create a ripple effect that extends far beyond our individual properties, inspiring others to follow suit and shaping a rental market that is fair, inclusive, and sustainable.

So, dear reader, I invite you to join me in reshaping the narrative surrounding landlords. Let us challenge the stereotypes, dispel the myths, and pave the way for a new era of ethical property management. Together, we can create a future where being a landlord is not an act of exploitation, but a commitment to serving our communities and fostering social progress.

Being a landlord is a major responsibility. As a property owner renting to tenants, you hold power over their housing situation and quality of life. This makes it imperative to act ethically in your role as a landlord, treating tenants fairly, respecting their rights, and maintaining properties to a safe and habitable standard.

This book provides a comprehensive guide to upholding the highest ethical principles as a landlord. It covers all aspects of the landlord-tenant relationship through an ethical lens, from screening prospective tenants in a non-discriminatory manner to protecting their privacy and security once they move in. You'll learn best practices for property maintenance, dealing with requests and complaints, conducting inspections, and properly handling terminations or evictions if absolutely necessary.

Beyond just following the letter of landlord-tenant laws, this book encourages going further to create a positive rental experience aligned with ethical values. This means being transparent in all dealings, treating tenants with respect and compassion, and considering the human impact of your actions and policies. Ethical landlords also strive to keep rents affordable, provide stability and cooperate with efforts to develop healthy, sustainable communities.

Whether you're a first-time accidental landlord or a professional property manager, this guide provides a moral framework to ensure you uphold your obligations to tenants while protecting your investment. True success as a landlord means not just financial return, but peace of mind in running an ethical business that has a positive impact. With a diligent commitment to doing the right thing, you can operate profitably while being a force for good in your community.

Being an ethical landlord requires an ongoing process of education, introspection and constant improvement. This book aims to be a catalyst for that journey, providing principles and practices you can apply to your unique situation. The road isn't always easy, but doing your best to "sleep well at night" by holding yourself to high ethical standards pays dividends through positive relationships with tenants built on mutual understanding and respect.

Are you ready to become a beacon of ethical stewardship in the rental market? Let us embark on this transformative journey together, and discover the immense power we hold to create positive change, one property at a time. Welcome to "The Complete Ethical Landlord."

Chapter 1: The Importance of Ethical Landlordship

Ethical Principles for Landlords

As a landlord committed to ethical practices, my foremost objective is to cultivate a positive and harmonious living environment for my tenants, while simultaneously ensuring the profitability and success of my rental properties. In this chapter, we will dig into the essential ethical principles that should govern the decision-making and interactions between landlords and tenants.

1. Upholding Tenant's Rights:

Respecting tenant's rights constitutes a fundamental ethical principle that should underpin all interactions within the landlord-tenant relationship. As a landlord, it is crucial to recognize and uphold the rights of tenants, which encompass privacy, a safe and habitable living space, and freedom from discrimination. By acknowledging and prioritizing these rights, a solid foundation is established for a healthy and equitable landlord-tenant relationship, fostering trust and mutual respect.

To ensure the preservation of tenant's rights, it is imperative for landlords to establish transparent and unequivocal policies regarding tenant privacy, property maintenance, and adherence to fair housing practices. By openly communicating these policies to tenants and consistently adhering to them, landlords can demonstrate their commitment to upholding ethical standards in their decision-making processes.

2. Fair and Transparent Rental Practices:

Another critical ethical principle for landlords is to engage in fair and transparent rental practices. This encompasses setting reasonable rental rates that align with the market value, ensuring equal treatment for all applicants, and providing unambiguous and comprehensive lease agreements.

When establishing rental rates, it is my objective to strike a balance between achieving a fair return on my investment and providing affordable housing options for tenants. Through thorough market research and consistent evaluation of local rental trends, I am able to ascertain that my rental rates are competitive and reflective of the property's value.

Additionally, I firmly believe in equal treatment for all applicants and tenants, irrespective of their race, color, religion, sex, national origin, familial status, or disability. I maintain strict adherence to fair housing laws and guidelines, and ensure that my tenant selection and application processes are solely based on objective criteria, such as income, credit history, and rental references.

Lastly, I recognize the significance of providing clear and comprehensive lease agreements. These contracts outline the rights and obligations of both the landlord and tenant, establishing a framework for a successful tenancy. By ensuring that the terms and conditions of the lease agreement are fair, easily comprehensible, and readily accessible to tenants, I create an environment that fosters open communication and minimizes the potential for misunderstandings.

3. Timely and Responsive Communication:

Effective and open communication is pivotal in cultivating a healthy and ethical landlord-tenant relationship. As a responsible landlord, I place great emphasis on prompt and responsive communication with my tenants.

I am cognizant that tenants may have concerns, queries, or requests that warrant attention. By promptly addressing these issues and providing clear explanations or resolutions, I am able to build trust and instill confidence in my tenants, assuring them that their needs are being acknowledged and attended to.

Responsive communication also extends to emergency situations. I ensure that my tenants have access to explicit instructions and reliable contact information in case of emergencies, thereby guaranteeing their safety and well-being at all times.

4. Diligent Property Maintenance and Repairs:

Ethical landlords prioritize property maintenance and repairs to ensure a safe and habitable living environment for their tenants. Regular property inspections, proactive maintenance, and timely repairs are indispensable in upholding this ethical principle.

I schedule regular inspections to identify potential issues before they escalate into significant problems. By promptly addressing concerns such as leaks, faulty appliances, or structural defects, I can intervene proactively and prevent any inconvenience or discomfort for my tenants.

Furthermore, I understand the value of proactive maintenance. Routine tasks such as gutter cleaning, lawn care, and HVAC system checks contribute to the preservation of my properties' condition and value, ultimately benefiting both my tenants and myself.

When repairs are necessary, I respond promptly and professionally. Whether it involves fixing a leaky faucet or addressing a major issue, I prioritize the well-being and satisfaction of my tenants. Quick turnaround times and effective communication during the repair process ensure that my tenants feel heard, supported, and well-cared for.

5. Consideration for Tenants' Financial Well-being:

An ethical landlord appreciates the impact of affordability on tenants' financial well-being. While maintaining a profitable rental business is important, equal emphasis is placed on being considerate of tenants' financial circumstances and striving to provide affordable housing options.

I regularly review my rental rates to ensure their competitiveness and alignment with local market trends. I also consider offering flexible lease terms, such as longer durations or rent concessions, for long-term tenants and those experiencing temporary financial difficulties.

Furthermore, I prioritize cost-saving initiatives that benefit both my tenants and the environment. Investments in energy-efficient appliances, implementation of recycling programs, and exploration of sustainable practices contribute to reduced utility expenses and environmental impact for my tenants.

The core ethical principles outlined in this chapter provide a framework for landlords to cultivate and maintain healthy, mutually beneficial relationships with their tenants. By respecting tenant's rights, engaging in fair rental practices, fostering open communication, prioritizing property maintenance and repairs, and considering tenants' financial well-being, ethical landlords lay the foundations for successful and fulfilling landlord-tenant partnerships.

Building Trust With Tenants

Over the course of my experience as a landlord, I have recognized that one of the most critical factors in achieving success in this profession is the establishment of trust with tenants. Trust forms the foundation for a harmonious and mutually beneficial landlord-tenant relationship, requiring meticulous attention and consistent effort. In this chapter, I will discuss a range of effective strategies that I have discovered for cultivating trust with tenants. These strategies encompass the domains of effective communication, transparency, and equitable treatment.

Effective communication stands as a central pillar of trust-building with tenants. It is paramount to establish unambiguous lines of communication from the outset of the landlord-tenant relationship. This can be achieved by stipulating expectations and boundaries pertaining to communication methods, response times, and preferred channels of interactions. For instance, I furnish my tenants with my contact information and clarify the most efficient means of reaching me in the event of emergencies or any other concerns that may arise.

In conjunction with setting expectations, it is crucial to exhibit responsiveness and accessibility in addressing the concerns and inquiries of tenants. Swiftly returning phone calls and emails, as well as actively listening to tenants' needs, signal that their concerns are highly regarded and esteemed. I exert deliberate effort to be readily available to my tenants, even if it necessitates modifying my schedule. This accessibility fosters trust and offers tenants the reassurance that I am available whenever they require assistance.

Transparency serves as another pivotal element in cultivating trust with tenants. By upholding transparency, landlords foster an atmosphere of candidness and integrity, which is conducive to trust. This can be achieved by disseminating unambiguous and straightforward information to tenants regarding lease terms, rental policies, and any modifications that may transpire throughout their tenancy. I make certain that my tenants possess a comprehensive understanding of the rental agreement, including all pertinent regulations and stipulations. This transparency not only engenders clear expectations but also mitigates the occurrence of misunderstandings and potential conflicts in the future.

Additionally, I take the view that transparency should be maintained with regard to maintenance and repair matters. Tenants genuinely appreciate being apprised of the measures being undertaken to address reported issues. Hence, I make it a priority to keep tenants informed concerning the progress of repairs and provide them with a realistic timeframe for resolution. Such transparency underscores my commitment to their comfort and well-being within the property.

Evidently, fair treatment is of paramount importance in nurturing trust with tenants. Ensuring that all tenants are treated with impartiality and respect engenders an environment where trust can thrive. Fair treatment encompasses unbiased tenant selection, offering equal opportunities to prospective renters, and equitable enforcement of lease provisions. I firmly believe in treating each tenant as an individual, duly considering their circumstances and needs when making decisions affecting them. By consistently demonstrating impartiality and fairness in my interactions with tenants, I establish an atmosphere of trust and mutual respect.

Moreover, I make it a priority to address concerns or disputes in an impartial and objective manner. This entails attentively listening to both sides of a given issue and reaching a resolution that is equitable and satisfactory for all parties involved. Through the demonstration of fairness in conflict resolution, I ensure that tenants feel heard and validated.

Cultivating trust with tenants is indispensable for cultivating successful and gratifying landlord-tenant relationships.

Strategies such as effective communication, transparency, and equitable treatment contribute significantly to the development of trust and the creation of a positive rental experience for both parties. Through dutiful implementation of these strategies, I have been able to foster a robust sense of trust with my tenants, thereby facilitating enduring and mutually advantageous relationships. As an ethical landlord, the cultivation of trust holds a central position within my business practices, and I persistently strive to enhance and refine these strategies to offer my tenants the optimum rental experience possible.

The Impact of Ethical Landlordship on Tenant Retention

As a landlord committed to ethical practices, I have always upheld the belief that treating tenants with fairness and respect is not only morally right but also crucial for the success of a rental business. In this section, we will explore the topic of tenant retention in greater depth and examine how ethical landlordship can significantly impact the ability to retain tenants.

Analyzing Ethical Practices:

It is common for many landlords to overlook the influence of their actions on tenant satisfaction, often prioritizing profit maximization above all else. However, I have come to recognize that by adopting ethical practices, landlords can create a positive environment that not only attracts but also retains tenants in the long term. It is imperative to fully comprehend the true meaning of ethical landlordship, which encompasses various elements such as transparency, effective communication, property maintenance, fair treatment, and respect for tenants' rights.

Enhancing Tenant Satisfaction:

One of the primary advantages of ethical landlordship is its ability to enhance tenant satisfaction. When tenants feel appreciated, respected, and heard, they are more inclined to remain in a property for an extended period. By establishing clear and open lines of communication, promptly addressing tenant concerns, and involving tenants in decision-making processes, landlords can establish trust and foster loyalty. Furthermore, ethical practices also involve providing safe and well-maintained properties, which contribute to overall tenant satisfaction.

Building a Sense of Community:

Based on my experience, cultivating a sense of community among tenants also plays a pivotal role in tenant retention. Ethical landlords understand the significance of creating shared spaces, organizing community events, and promoting a harmonious living environment. By encouraging positive interactions between tenants, landlords can cultivate a sense of belonging and encourage long-term tenancy.

Fair Pricing and Rent Increases:

Another ethical practice that has a considerable impact on tenant retention is fair pricing and reasonable rent increases.

While it is essential for landlords to earn a fair return on their investment, it is equally important to strike a balance that takes into account the financial well-being of tenants. Adopting ethical practices with regards to rent increases, such as providing advanced notice and considering the affordability of tenants, can lead to higher tenant satisfaction and a greater likelihood of tenant retention.

Managing Conflict:

Conflict between landlords and tenants is inevitable, but how it is handled can significantly influence tenant retention. Ethical landlords approach conflict resolution with empathy, fairness, and professionalism. By actively listening to tenants' concerns, seeking mutually satisfactory resolutions, and ensuring prompt resolution of disputes, landlords can create an environment where tenants feel valued and respected. This not only resolves immediate conflicts but also strengthens the landlord-tenant relationship.

Benefits for Landlords:

While the primary focus of ethical practices may be tenant satisfaction and retention, it is important to acknowledge the benefits that come with it for landlords as well. Increased tenant retention rates lead to a more stable rental income stream, reduced vacancy periods, and lower turnover costs. Ethical practices also contribute to a positive reputation in the rental market, attracting potential tenants who value ethical landlordship. Additionally, by proactively maintaining properties, landlords can increase their value and decrease long-term expenses.

Ethical landlordship has a profound impact on tenant retention rates. By examining and implementing ethical practices such as transparent communication, cultivating a sense of community, fair pricing and rent increases, conflict resolution, and prioritizing tenant satisfaction, landlords can elevate their rental business. Ethical practices not only benefit tenants but also provide long-term advantages for landlords, ultimately creating a mutually beneficial situation. As an ethical landlord, I firmly believe that by prioritizing the well-being of tenants, we can cultivate a thriving and sustainable rental business for years to come.

Ethical Approaches to Rent Collection

As landlords, it is our primary responsibility to collect rent from our tenants. Although this task may appear straightforward, I have acquired knowledge throughout the years that there are various ethical approaches that can be employed to make this process more compassionate and considerate. In this chapter, we will examine different ethical approaches to rent collection, with a focus on offering flexible payment options, understanding financial hardships, and fostering open dialogue with tenants.

1. Flexible Payment Options:

When it comes to rent collection, one of the initial ethical considerations should be the provision of flexible payment options to our tenants. By recognizing that each individual's financial situation is unique, we can help alleviate the burden of paying rent on time. One approach that I have embraced is allowing tenants to select from monthly, bi-weekly, or weekly payment plans, based on their income schedule. This not only ensures consistent rent payment but also empowers tenants to align their payments with their cash flow.

Furthermore, I have implemented a system where tenants can request temporary payment plans if they encounter unforeseen financial difficulties. By granting this level of flexibility and understanding, we can cultivate a positive tenant-landlord relationship founded on trust and compassion.

2. Understanding Financial Hardships:

Another ethical approach to rent collection involves developing a deep understanding of the financial hardships that tenants may face. Life can be unpredictable, and circumstances such as job loss or medical emergencies can significantly impact an individual's ability to pay rent on time. Therefore, it is our duty as landlords to demonstrate empathy and support during these challenging times.

For instance, I have established a policy that enables tenants to submit supporting documentation for their financial hardships, such as medical bills, termination notices, or unemployment records. By carefully reviewing these documents, I can gain a comprehensive understanding of the situation and collaborate with the tenant to find a suitable solution. This approach not only helps prevent unnecessary evictions but also showcases a genuine concern for the well-being of tenants.

3. Fostering Open Dialogue:

One of the most pivotal aspects of ethical rent collection is the cultivation of open dialogue with our tenants. Establishing effective communication channels facilitates trust and understanding among all parties involved. Consistently checking in with tenants and making ourselves available to listen to their concerns creates a supportive environment that encourages open conversations.

To ensure that tenants feel at ease discussing their financial situations, I have utilized various communication methods. For instance, I have implemented a secure online portal where tenants can communicate their payment challenges or concerns. Additionally, I have scheduled regular meetings with tenants to address any difficulties they may be experiencing and work collaboratively to find a solution. By fostering this open dialogue, we can address potential issues before they escalate and maintain a positive landlord-tenant relationship.

4. Offering Financial Education and Resources:

Lastly, an ethical approach to rent collection entails educating tenants about financial management and providing accessible resources. Many individuals may not have received formal education in personal finance, and it is our responsibility as landlords to help bridge this knowledge gap.

To achieve this objective, I have collaborated with local financial institutions and community organizations to facilitate workshops and seminars on topics such as budgeting, saving, and credit management. Additionally, I have compiled a list of resources, including government assistance programs and non-profit organizations, that tenants can utilize if they require financial support. By offering these educational opportunities and resources, we empower our tenants to enhance their financial literacy and fulfill their rent obligations more effectively.

Ethical approaches to rent collection are fundamental to being a compassionate and understanding landlord. By implementing flexible payment options, understanding financial hardships, fostering open dialogue, and offering financial education and resources, we can establish a harmonious and mutually beneficial relationship with our tenants. It is through compassion, empathy, and an adaptable mindset that we can build a strong community and ensure the well-being of all parties involved in the rental process.

Balancing Profitability and Ethical Practices

Since embarking on the journey as a landlord, I have encountered numerous individuals who hold the belief that ethical landlordship and profitability are mutually exclusive. This misconception has persisted in the industry for an extended period, often leading landlords to compromise their ethical principles in the pursuit of financial success. However, the truth is that it is indeed possible to strike a balance between ethical practices and profitability. The purpose of this chapter is to challenge the notion that these two concepts are incompatible and provide valuable insights on how to navigate the delicate balance between ethics and financial success.

As a landlord, my ethical standpoint has always centered around treating my tenants with respect and ensuring their well-being. I firmly believe that my responsibility goes beyond merely providing them with a place to live; it is also my duty to create a safe and comfortable environment that allows them to thrive. Consequently, I have implemented a range of practices that prioritize their needs and guarantee their satisfaction, without compromising the profitability of my endeavors.

One crucial step in dispelling this misconception is to redefine the concept of profitability. Contrary to popular belief, profitability does not require maximizing every possible cent at the expense of one's ethical responsibility. While it is undeniably important to generate a reasonable return on investment, it must never come at the cost of exploiting or disregarding the rights of tenants. By viewing profitability as a means to sustain and enhance ethical practices, landlords can align their financial goals with their ethical principles.

To strike a balance between ethical practices and profitability, it is crucial to establish a solid foundation through intensive research and a comprehensive understanding of the local housing market. By meticulously analyzing the demand for rental properties, landlords can identify areas where their expertise can fulfill a genuine need in a responsible manner. This approach not only ensures a consistent stream of income but also allows landlords to provide a service that caters to the needs of tenants ethically. This empathetic approach to the business can lead to long-term, sustainable profitability.

Furthermore, it is imperative to address the misconception that ethical practices require landlords to forego financial success. In reality, maintaining ethical standards can actually enhance profitability. For example, ensuring regular property maintenance and promptly addressing repairs not only creates a pleasant living environment for tenants but also preserves the property's long-term value. By prioritizing the well-being of tenants, landlords can cultivate a positive reputation in the community, attracting high-quality tenants who are willing to pay a premium for a well-managed property.

Moreover, adopting ethical practices can also lead to reduced turnover rates among tenants. When tenants feel valued and respected, they are more inclined to renew their leases, saving landlords the time and resources typically required in finding new tenants. Additionally, by fostering open lines of communication and promptly addressing any concerns or complaints, landlords can further enhance tenant satisfaction, resulting in longer and more profitable tenancies.

One common challenge in balancing profitability and ethical practices is navigating the complexities of legal and regulatory frameworks. Landlords must possess a comprehensive understanding of local laws governing rental properties to ensure that their practices conform to legal requirements and protect their tenants' rights. This encompasses familiarity with rent control policies, fair housing laws, and eviction procedures, among other crucial aspects. By operating within the bounds of the law, landlords can uphold ethical practices while safeguarding their financial interests.

In certain instances, ethical practices may necessitate additional investments or expenses. For example, implementing sustainable features within rental properties can reduce energy consumption and promote environmental responsibility. While these upgrades may require a higher initial investment, they can result in long-term cost savings and attract tenants who value environmentally conscious living. By carefully evaluating the potential returns on these investments, landlords can make informed decisions that serve both ethical and financial objectives.

Timing also plays a pivotal role in achieving a balance between ethical practices and profitability. It is important to strike a balance, ensuring that rent prices are fair and accurately reflect local market conditions. While landlords have the right to earn a return on their investment, setting excessively high rents can exploit tenants and cause financial strain. Conducting regular assessments of the market and staying informed about changes in the housing landscape allows landlords to adjust their rental rates responsibly, balancing both profitability and ethical considerations.

Dispelling the misconception that ethical landlordship is incompatible with profitability is essential for landlords aspiring to establish themselves as ethical stewards of the rental industry. By redefining the concept of profitability and understanding that ethical practices can enhance financial success, landlords can strike a careful balance between these seemingly opposing forces. Thorough research, understanding the local market, and aligning financial goals with ethical principles are all essential elements in achieving sustainable profitability while upholding ethical practices. With diligence and a commitment to the well-being of tenants, every landlord can serve as a shining example of how ethics and profitability can coexist.

Ethical Property Investments

As landlords, our commitment to ethical practices should extend beyond just the day-to-day operations and management of rental properties. The decisions we make regarding property acquisitions, renovations, and upgrades can have a profound impact on our ability to uphold ethical standards while ensuring long-term profitability.

When considering the purchase of a new investment property, it is essential to evaluate not only the financial viability but also the ethical implications. Properties in disadvantaged or underserved communities may present opportunities to provide safe, affordable housing options while promoting sustainable development and community revitalization efforts. By carefully researching the local housing needs and working closely with community stakeholders, ethical landlords can make informed investment decisions that align with their values and contribute to positive societal change.

Furthermore, the types of renovations and upgrades undertaken on existing properties can significantly influence both ethical goals and profitability. Investing in energy-efficient appliances, eco-friendly building materials, and sustainable features not only aligns with environmental responsibility but can also result in long-term cost savings through reduced utility expenses. These investments can enhance the property's appeal to environmentally conscious tenants, potentially commanding higher rental rates and improving long-term asset value.

Accessibility and inclusivity should also be at the forefront when considering property improvements. Renovations that promote universal design principles, such as installing ramps, widening doorways, and incorporating accessible features, can ensure that rental units are welcoming to individuals with disabilities. Not only is this an ethical imperative, but it can also expand the potential tenant pool and contribute to a more diverse and inclusive community.

Ethical landlords may also consider investing in community spaces, shared amenities, or social programs that foster a sense of community and enhance the overall living experience for tenants. While these investments may require additional upfront costs, they can pay dividends in the form of increased tenant satisfaction, reduced turnover rates, and a positive reputation that attracts high-quality, long-term tenants.

It is important to note that while some ethical property investments may initially appear to be more costly, they can often lead to long-term cost savings and increased profitability. By carefully evaluating the potential returns on these investments and considering the broader societal and environmental impacts, landlords can make informed decisions that align with their ethical principles while ensuring the financial sustainability of their business.

By integrating ethical considerations into property investment decisions, landlords can demonstrate their commitment to creating not just profitable ventures but also positive, lasting impacts on the communities they serve. This holistic approach to property ownership and management is the hallmark of truly ethical landlordship.

Chapter 2: Creating a Positive Rental Experience

Maintaining High-Quality Rental Properties

Ensuring regular property maintenance is a paramount responsibility for landlords who aim to uphold high standards. This practice serves as the foundation for providing well-maintained rental properties. In the realm of maintenance, preventive measures are always superior to reactive ones. By implementing regular maintenance routines and checklists, landlords can keep their properties in optimal condition, thus minimizing the need for extensive repairs in the long term.

Scheduled inspections serve as an effective means of staying up to date with property maintenance. These inspections enable landlords to identify any maintenance issues at an early stage and address them promptly. From assessing potential leakages in pipes to inspecting electrical systems, each aspect of the property is thoroughly examined to ensure everything is in proper working order. Furthermore, these inspections allow landlords to assess the overall condition of the rental property and identify areas that may require improvement or upgrades.

To facilitate prompt repairs, I have established a system allowing tenants to easily report any maintenance issues encountered. Whether it be a leaking faucet, broken window, or malfunctioning appliance, tenants are encouraged to promptly notify me of these problems. Recognizing the significance of acknowledging and prioritizing these requests, I display a commitment to providing a safe and comfortable environment for tenants. Promptly addressing repairs not only prevents minor issues from escalating but also showcases a dedication to tenants' well-being.

To instill safety and comfort in my rental properties, I have implemented several measures. Firstly, I ensure that all properties adhere to safety regulations and standards. Features such as smoke detectors, carbon monoxide alarms, and sufficient fire exits are consistently implemented to prioritize safety. Regular inspections are conducted to verify the functionality of these safety measures.

Furthermore, efforts have been made to enhance the comfort of the living spaces. This includes providing proper insulation to maintain optimal temperatures, installing efficient heating, ventilation, and air conditioning systems, as well as ensuring the good condition of plumbing and electrical systems. Additionally, I maintain clean and well-maintained common areas, laundry facilities, and ample parking spaces. These endeavors ensure tenants can enjoy a comfortable and stress-free living experience.

Based on my experience as a conscientious landlord, I have observed the positive impact of maintaining high-quality rental properties. This not only attracts responsible and reliable tenants but also fosters a sense of pride and satisfaction for both myself and the tenants alike. By consistently fulfilling my role as a meticulous landlord, I establish trust with my tenants, fostering long-term tenancies and ultimately yielding profitability within the rental business.

By highlighting the importance of regular property maintenance, addressing repairs promptly, and providing safe and comfortable living environments for tenants, I aspire to inspire other landlords to adopt ethical practices within their own rental businesses. Through collective efforts, we can contribute to the enhancement of the rental industry and ensure tenants have access to exceptional housing options.

Effective Tenant Screening Techniques

Background checks are an indispensable tool in tenant screening, enabling me to gather vital information regarding an individual's criminal record, eviction history, and prior addresses. To perform a comprehensive background check, I collaborate with a reputable screening agency specialized in compiling this data. By partnering with experts well-versed in the legal and privacy aspects of background checks, I can guarantee the lawful acquisition and dissemination of all information.

Upon obtaining consent from prospective tenants, I initiate the background check process. This entails furnishing the screening agency with requisite personal details, such as full name, date of birth, and social security number. While I acknowledge the apprehensions some individuals may have in divulging such sensitive data, I reassure them that their information would be handled securely and exclusively employed for screening purposes.

Following the completion of the background check, I meticulously review the findings, paying careful attention to any indicators of potential risks. For instance, if a tenant has a history of violence or drug-related offenses, it raises concerns about the safety of the property and the welfare of other residents. In such instances, I typically decline the application in order to maintain a safe living environment for all occupants.

Another pivotal facet of tenant screening is evaluating the creditworthiness of prospective tenants. Credit assessments provide valuable insights into an individual's financial dependability and stability. To conduct a credit evaluation, I acquire the applicant's consent to access their credit report, which encompasses their credit score, payment history, and outstanding debts. This step not only assists me in gauging the applicant's ability to fulfill their financial obligations but also guards against potential financial burdens on my properties.

I acknowledge that a subpar credit score does not necessarily indicate an irresponsible tenant. Consequently, I adopt a holistic approach when evaluating an applicant's creditworthiness. I consider factors such as the rationale behind any negative entries on their credit report, their present employment status and income, and any active measures they are taking to improve their financial circumstances. By taking these factors into consideration, I am able to obtain a comprehensive understanding of the applicant's financial capabilities and make a well-informed decision based on their overall financial profile.

Reference verification is yet another critical step in tenant screening. This encompasses reaching out to the applicant's former landlords or property managers to solicit feedback and assess the applicant's rental history. During these conversations, I strive to obtain information pertaining to the applicant's conduct as a tenant, their punctuality in rent payments, their adherence to lease terms, and their overall sense of responsibility. I approach these inquiries with empathy and respect, mindful that previous landlords might be occupied or hesitant to share information. I assure them that their input carries immense value and will significantly influence my decision-making process.

By discussing these various tenant screening techniques with potential tenants, I foster an atmosphere of transparency and trust. I provide detailed explanations of each step and encourage applicants to raise any queries or voice concerns they may have. This open dialogue ensures that prospective tenants comprehend, to the best of their ability, the rationale behind each screening method. Furthermore, I emphasize that while these methods may appear invasive, they are indispensable for establishing a secure and protected living environment for all residents.

The implementation of effective tenant screening techniques is imperative for ethical property owners like myself. Background checks, credit evaluations, and reference verification serve as invaluable tools in assessing the suitability of prospective tenants. By performing thorough and compliant screenings, I guarantee that I am entrusting my rental properties to responsible and trustworthy individuals. These techniques ultimately contribute to the success and long-term sustainability of my rental business, while also safeguarding the well-being and contentment of all residents.

Resolving Tenant Issues and Disputes Fairly

Step 1: Active Listening and Empathy

The initial step in fairly resolving tenant issues and disputes is to engage in active listening and demonstrate empathy for their situation. Whenever a tenant approaches me with a complaint or problem, I prioritize giving them my full attention and expressing sincere compassion. This approach establishes trust and encourages tenants to share the details of their concerns.

Step 2: Open Communication

After tenants have expressed their concerns, it is crucial to maintain open lines of communication throughout the resolution process. I encourage tenants to be forthright and transparent about their issues, and in turn, I reciprocate this honesty by sharing relevant information and providing regular updates on progress.

Step 3: Gathering Information

To ensure fair and informed decision-making, I dedicate time to gathering all pertinent information related to the tenant's issue or dispute. This involves conducting interviews with all parties involved, reviewing relevant documentation, and examining the property for potential evidence.

Step 4: Assessing the Situation

Once all necessary information has been gathered, a careful assessment of the situation is carried out to comprehend the underlying causes and factors contributing to the issue or dispute. This assessment involves considering the rights and responsibilities of both the tenant and the landlord, as outlined in the lease agreement and in compliance with local laws and regulations.

Step 5: Considering Mediation

In numerous cases, disputes can be effectively resolved through mediation. It is in this stage that all parties are brought together, including the tenant, any relevant witnesses, and myself as the landlord, to facilitate a constructive discussion and explore possible resolutions. As the mediator, I maintain impartiality and guide the conversation towards reaching a mutually agreed-upon solution.

Step 6: Exploring Potential Solutions

During the mediation process, I actively encourage tenants and other involved parties to brainstorm potential solutions to the issue or dispute. This might involve suggesting compromises, seeking input from experts or professionals, or exploring alternative options that meet the needs and preferences of both parties.

Step 7: Reaching a Fair Resolution

Once potential solutions have been thoroughly explored, I collaborate with the involved parties to reach a fair resolution that considers everyone's rights and interests. I ensure that the resolution is realistic and feasible, and I document it in writing to provide clarity and prevent future disputes.

Step 8: Implementing the Resolution

Following the attainment of a fair resolution, it is essential to promptly and effectively implement the agreed-upon solution. This may encompass specific actions such as property repairs or modifications, lease term adjustments, or providing the tenant with compensation for any damages or inconveniences experienced.

Step 9: Follow-Up and Feedback

Following the resolution of an issue or dispute, I sustain open communication with the tenant to ensure their satisfaction with the solution and that any remaining concerns are addressed. I also encourage tenants to provide feedback on the resolution process, as it enables me to continuously enhance my approach to fairly handling tenant issues and disputes.

Step 10: Documentation and Learning

Throughout the entire process of resolving tenant issues and disputes, I meticulously maintain detailed records of all communications, actions taken, and outcomes. This documentation serves not only as a point of reference for the future but also as a valuable learning tool. By reviewing past cases and learning from any errors or deficiencies, I continuously refine my approach to ensure fairness and ethical conduct in all future tenant interactions.

Tthe fair resolution of tenant issues and disputes necessitates active listening, open communication, and a dedication to impartiality. By following this comprehensive guide, I strive to foster open communication and conflict resolution, thereby creating a positive and harmonious living environment for both tenants and landlords. An ethical landlord prioritizes fairness and actively works towards resolving disputes in a manner that takes into account the rights and interests of all parties involved.

Tenant Communication Best Practices

Effective communication is the bedrock of a positive landlord-tenant relationship. Establishing clear channels and protocols for communication ensures tenants feel heard, respected and kept informed. Based on my experience, both as a landlord and previous tenant, I recognize just how impactful open communication can be.

When I was renting an apartment years ago, I vividly recall coming home one evening to find my front door wide open and a maintenance crew halfway through replacing my bathtub. Understandably, I was shocked and upset to discover strangers in my home unannounced and my bathroom in disarray, with my personal toiletry items handled. This situation could have been avoided entirely had there been proper communication from my landlord about the scheduled work.

That experience crystallized for me the importance of transparent and timely communication with tenants about anything impacting their living spaces. As a landlord now, I have implemented specific best practices:

Provide Advanced Notice: For any non-emergency repairs, renovations or contractors entering a rental unit, I ensure tenants receive written notice at least 24-48 hours in advance per legal requirements. This allows them to prepare and plan accordingly.

Establish Preferred Communication Channels: At move-in, I consult with each tenant on their preferred methods of communication (email, text, phone call) for different situations to prevent miscommunication.

Set Clear Response Timelines: I provide tenants with my contact information and commitment to responding to all non-emergency inquiries within 24-48 business hours to promote transparency.

Outline Emergency Protocols: Tenants receive clear instructions on who to contact and what procedures to follow in case of urgent maintenance emergencies like floods, fires or break-ins.

Provide Regular Updates: For any major repairs or construction projects, I ensure tenants remain updated on progress, estimated completion timelines and any other pertinent details through periodic emails or calls.

Be Proactive, Not Reactive: Rather than waiting for tenants to raise concerns, I aim to proactively communicate about community updates, policy changes, planned capital improvements and more.

By prioritizing open and respectful communication following these protocols, I establish trust and make tenants feel their landlord is transparent, organized and considers their need for information. This strengthens our relationship and ensures surprises like coming home to an unexpectedly renovated bathroom do not occur.

Taking the extra steps to communicate effectively prevents confusion, respects tenants' rights to privacy and peace of mind in their home, and allows for a harmonious rental experience. Implementing robust communication practices is a hallmark of ethical landlordship.

Promoting Diversity and Inclusion in Rental Practices

One of the fundamental elements in promoting diversity and inclusion in rental practices involves the establishment and enforcement of fair housing policies. These policies are designed to prevent housing discrimination based on protected classes, such as race, color, religion, sex, familial status, national origin, and disability. As a conscientious landlord, it is incumbent upon me to be well-informed about these policies and ensure their integration throughout all aspects of my rental business.

To ensure equitable treatment, it is imperative to adopt an impartial and unbiased tenant selection process. When evaluating prospective tenants, it is essential to solely focus on their qualifications, including their creditworthiness, rental history, and income. By making decisions solely based on objective criteria, I can mitigate the risk of inadvertently discriminating against individuals who belong to certain protected classes.

I exert considerable effort to combat discrimination in all its forms and actively strive to foster an inclusive rental community. In addition to adhering to fair housing policies, there are several proactive measures I can take to promote diversity and inclusion. For example, I actively seek out diverse marketing channels to reach a broad array of individuals. By advertising my rental properties in different communities and marketplaces, I enhance the likelihood of attracting a diverse pool of potential tenants.

Additionally, I prioritize educating myself and my staff on cultural sensitivity and awareness. It is important to be mindful of diverse cultural practices and traditions, ensuring that all tenants feel respected and comfortable in their living spaces. This may include understanding dietary restrictions, providing appropriate language support, and accommodating religious practices whenever feasible.

Another vital aspect of promoting diversity and inclusion is creating a sense of belonging and community among tenants. I plan and organize regular community events and activities that facilitate tenant interactions, the sharing of experiences and stories, and the formation of connections. By nurturing a sense of community, I aspire to dismantle any existing barriers and establish an environment where everyone feels valued and included.

Moreover, I remain committed to collaborating with local organizations that endorse diversity and inclusion initiatives. By partnering with these organizations, I can tap into their resources and expertise to further enhance my rental practices. This may entail participating in workshops or training sessions to deepen my understanding of diversity and inclusivity, as well as accessing resources that facilitate the connection with diverse tenants.

While promoting diversity and inclusion in rental practices demands continuous effort and dedication, the benefits are far-reaching. It not only cultivates a more harmonious living environment for tenants but also positively contributes to the overall community. Embracing diversity and inclusion can foster a stronger sense of social cohesion, increased tolerance, and opportunities for personal growth and learning.Aas an ethical landlord, I am unwavering in my commitment to promoting diversity and inclusion within rental practices. Through the implementation of fair housing policies, the enforcement of equal treatment, the active combatting of discrimination, the fostering of a sense of community, and the collaboration with local organizations, I endeavor to establish an inclusive rental environment where all individuals feel valued and respected. By embracing diversity, I firmly believe that we can nurture a more robust, vibrant rental community that benefits all stakeholders involved.

Enhancing Tenant Well-being and

Community Engagement

As a conscientious landlord, I firmly believe in the pivotal role that a strong sense of community plays in fostering a thriving and harmonious living environment. Over the course of my extensive experience in the real estate industry, I have observed firsthand the transformative effects that cultivating a robust community spirit among tenants can have. This not only enhances the individual well-being of residents but also contributes to the overall vitality of the property.

In today's fast-paced modern world, where societal isolation and disconnection are pervasive, it is imperative that landlords comprehend and address the need for community connection. Residents who feel a sense of belonging are not only happier and healthier but are also more likely to remain in their homes for extended periods of time. With this recognition, I have taken purposeful measures to establish an environment that actively promotes social interaction and communal engagement.

One impactful avenue to foster a sense of community is through the provision of amenities and services oriented towards the well-being of tenants. Research reveals that access to recreational facilities, fitness centers, and communal spaces can have a significantly favorable impact on both mental and physical health. Mindful of this, I have made investments in the creation of well-designed common areas, such as lounges, gardens, and fitness rooms, where residents can convene, relax, and partake in meaningful conversations with their neighbors.

Furthermore, I have collaborated with local organizations and professionals to offer enriching services to my tenants. These services encompass wellness workshops, financial management resources, and even art therapy sessions. Through the provision of these resources, my aim is to empower tenants to lead fulfilling lives and build stronger connections within the community.

In addition to amenities and services, fostering community engagement necessitates active participation from resident members. To promote this, I have implemented an array of initiatives designed to underscore the significance of tenant involvement in community activities. Regular community meetings serve as a platform for residents to voice their concerns, suggestions, and aspirations. By facilitating dialogue, collaboration, and the cultivation of a shared vision for the property, these gatherings offer an opportunity for active engagement.

To further facilitate sustained tenant participation, I have established a tenant-led community board responsible for planning and implementing various events and activities. This approach ensures that the interests, needs, and diversity of the residents are accounted for and represented. By engaging tenants in decision-making processes, they not only develop a sense of ownership but also forge a deeper connection to their living space.

To further integrate the lives of tenants with the wider community, I actively encourage partnerships with local businesses, charities, and volunteer organizations. Through coordinated endeavors, such as joint community projects involving food drives, fundraisers, and tree plantations, we create opportunities for residents to engage with their surroundings and contribute to the community that nurtures them. This not only heightens their sense of purpose but also forges stronger bonds between the property and the broader neighborhood.

Recognizing that community engagement is an ongoing journey rather than a destination, I continually seek feedback from tenants. Regular surveys, focus groups, and one-on-one conversations enable me to comprehend their evolving needs and aspirations. This continuous dialogue ensures that my efforts to enhance tenant well-being and community engagement remain relevant and meaningful.Eemphasizing the importance of fostering a sense of community among tenants, promoting well-being through amenities and services, and encouraging tenant participation in community activities are pivotal for landlords committed to ethical practices. Through investment in these aspects, I have personally witnessed the positive impact they have on the overall tenant experience. By creating an environment conducive to nurturing a sense of belonging, wherein individuals feel supported, connected, and engaged, not only do tenants benefit but a more vibrant and content community is formed. As an ethical landlord, I remain steadfast in my dedication to continually enhancing tenant well-being and community engagement, acutely aware that these efforts will yield lasting benefits for all who call my property home.

Connecting Tenants with Community Resources

As an ethical landlord, my responsibilities extend beyond simply providing quality housing - I also strive to support the overall well-being of my tenants. One way I demonstrate this commitment is by ensuring tenants have access to information on valuable community resources and support services.

No one is immune to the challenges life can bring, whether it is a temporary setback like job loss or more ongoing needs like mental health counseling, childcare assistance, or chronic illness support. When times get tough, being connected to the right resources can make a tremendous difference for individuals and families. By providing tenants with a centralized list of helpful local services, I aim to be a source of support if they ever need it.

The tenant resource guide I create covers a wide range of potential needs, including:

- Food insecurity resources like food banks, soup kitchens, grocery delivery

- Affordable healthcare services and clinics

- Childcare options and family support services

- Mental health counseling and therapy providers

- Substance abuse treatment programs

- Financial counseling and income assistance

- Affordable legal aid services

- Career centers and job search assistance

- Tutoring, after-school programs and educational resources

- Local transportation services for those without vehicles

Compiled from government websites, non-profits, community organizations and more, this curated list is shared with every new tenant during move-in. I make it clear that it is a judgment-free zone, and tenants can access the information as needed without any stigma or breaching their privacy.

For tenants who do experience hardship, this resource guide provides a gateway to get connected with groups and services that may help improve their situation. From crisis prevention to securing long-term stability, these organizations offer invaluable assistance. As a landlord, I cannot solve every problem, but I can point tenants in the right direction.

Additionally, I aim to foster a sense of community among my tenants themselves as sometimes they may be able to provide support too. I'll occasionally organize social gatherings or set up neighborhood communication channels where tenants can opt-in to ask for help with tasks like childcare swaps, grocery runs or even just a friendly check-in if they live alone.

While landlords may typically focus on the bricks and mortar, I believe cultivating connections to wider community resources demonstrates a more holistic commitment to tenants. By providing this guidance, I hope to not only ease potential burdens, but reinforce that tenants' well-being is a priority to me. A little bit of empathy can go a long way.

Chapter 3: Ethical Approaches to Rent Pricing

Market Research and Fair Rent Assessment

Market research is an essential aspect of maintaining a morally upright standing as a landlord. By comprehending the local rental market, one is able to gauge the supply and demand of rental properties within the area. This knowledge ultimately aids in setting rent prices that align with current market conditions, ensuring that they are realistic. Without conducting market research, there is a risk of either overpricing one's properties and struggling to secure tenants or underpricing them and suffering financial losses.

To effectively conduct market research, a range of resources and techniques are utilized. One of the initial steps involves analyzing rental listings within the local vicinity. By examining comparable properties, valuable insights into prevailing rental rates for similar units can be obtained. Factors such as property size, location, and amenities are carefully considered. Consequently, these factors enable informed decisions to be made regarding the pricing of one's own properties.

Moreover, it is prudent to regularly partake in local real estate events and establish a network with fellow landlords and property managers. Engaging in these discussions provides the landlord with valuable firsthand knowledge regarding emerging trends within the rental market. This knowledge allows for a better assessment of the demand for specific types of properties, empowering the landlord to make informed decisions regarding rental prices adjustment.

Another fruitful resource for market research is the utilization of online rental platforms. Such platforms furnish access to a vast array of rental data and analytics. Information regarding the performance of similar properties, duration of their presence on the market, and achieved rental prices can be gleaned from these resources. By meticulously analyzing such data, the landlord is capable of making calculated decisions regarding the pricing of their properties in a competitive manner.

In addition to market research, fair rent assessment carries equal importance. This practice ensures that a reasonable and justifiable sum is being charged for the properties on offer. Several factors are taken into account during this assessment that influence rental prices.

One of the foremost factors that bear weight in fair rent assessment is the location. Properties located in desirable neighborhoods that boast reputable schools, amenities, and good transportation links generally command higher rental fees. Conversely, properties situated in less sought-after areas may require lower rent rates in order to attract tenants. The landlord continually considers the location of their properties and adjusts rent prices accordingly.

The condition of the property is another determining factor in fair rent assessment. A well-maintained and renovated property typically warrants higher rents compared to those in disrepair. To ensure that properties are in optimal condition and can justify fair rental prices, the landlord consistently invests in the maintenance and enhancement of these properties.

The presence of amenities also plays a significant role in fair rent assessment. Properties that offer amenities such as parking spaces, laundry facilities, gym access, or outdoor spaces are often deemed more desirable, warranting higher rental rates. By providing such amenities, the landlord can attract quality tenants who value the convenience and added value that these amenities bring.

To guarantee fair rent assessment, the income levels and affordability of potential tenants are taken into consideration. Striking a balance between maximizing profits as a landlord and providing affordable housing options is crucial. Charging exorbitant rents may exclude potential tenants who cannot afford them, resulting in increased vacancies and financial instability.

By conducting market research and implementing fair rent assessment, the landlord is able to establish rent prices that are fair, competitive, and advantageous for both parties involved. This approach fosters a respectful and ethical relationship with tenants, whilst simultaneously maximizing profitability. As an ethical landlord, upholding the responsibility to ensure that rental prices reflect market conditions and consider the needs and affordability of tenants is of paramount importance.

Avoiding Rent Gouging and Exploitative

Practices

As a conscientious landlord, I am fully dedicated to ensuring fairness and affordability for my tenants. I recognize the detrimental effects of rent gouging and exploitative rent practices on individuals and communities, and firmly believe in taking proactive measures to address these issues.

Rent gouging, which refers to the practice of significantly increasing rents in response to high demand or low supply, negatively impacts tenants who are already struggling to find affordable housing. It exacerbates inequalities and forces vulnerable individuals and families out of their homes. Exploitative rent practices, such as imposing exorbitant fees or imposing unrealistic lease terms, further victimize tenants who may have limited resources and bargaining power.

When addressing the ethical implications of rent gouging and exploitative rent practices, it is crucial to consider the human aspect of the issue. Rent is not merely a financial transaction; it is the means by which people secure shelter and build their lives. By prioritizing profit over the well-being of tenants, landlords perpetuate injustices and contribute to societal inequalities. Therefore, it is imperative for ethical landlords to adopt alternative approaches that foster affordability and fairness in the rental market.

One alternative approach that can be implemented to mitigate rent gouging and exploitative rent practices is the establishment of rent control policies. Rent control is a mechanism in which the government sets limits on the annual rent increase that landlords can impose. These policies help stabilize rents and prevent sudden and unjustified increases that burden tenants. While critics argue that rent control may discourage investment in rental properties, it is important to strike a balance between profitability and social responsibility. For example, some cities have implemented rent stabilization measures that allow landlords to earn a reasonable return on their investment while protecting tenants.

Another alternative approach worth exploring is the implementation of affordable housing programs. These programs aim to increase the supply of affordable rental units in high-demand areas by offering subsidies or incentives to developers. By creating more affordable housing options, tenants are not only protected from rent gouging but are also more likely to secure stable, long-term housing. Ethical landlords can actively engage with these programs by partnering with affordable housing developers or offering their properties for affordable rental purposes. This benefits both tenants and the community as a whole.

Additionally, ethical landlords must prioritize transparent and fair rental practices. This includes providing clear and reasonable lease terms, openly communicating any rental increases or changes, and avoiding unreasonable fees. By ensuring transparency, landlords empower tenants to make informed decisions and protect themselves against exploitative practices. Moreover, ethical landlords should actively engage with tenants, establishing open lines of communication to promptly address any concerns or grievances. By fostering a respectful and collaborative relationship, ethical landlords can create a mutually beneficial environment where tenants feel valued and supported.

it is a fundamental responsibility of ethical landlords to address the ethical implications of rent gouging and exploitative rent practices. By prioritizing affordability and fairness, landlords can contribute to the well-being of their tenants and the community as a whole. The alternative approaches discussed in this chapter, such as rent control policies, affordable housing programs, and transparent rental practices, offer viable solutions to combat rent gouging and exploitation. Through proactive measures and a commitment to social responsibility, ethical landlords can make a meaningful difference in the lives of their tenants and help build a more equitable and just rental market.

Implementing Rent Increases Responsibly

One of the primary considerations when implementing rent increases is the affordability of housing for tenants. It is imperative to ensure that any increase in rent does not impose an excessive burden on tenants, particularly those who may already be facing financial difficulties. To address this concern, a deliberate approach is necessary, one that takes into account the income levels and financial circumstances of the tenants.

A step I consistently undertake before implementing rent increases is evaluating the financial position of my tenants. I assess whether the increase in rent would result in an unmanageable financial situation for them. This entails considering factors such as their income, expenses, and any additional financial obligations they may have. By conducting this assessment, I can determine the fairness and feasibility of a rent increase for my tenants.

Another significant consideration is the prevailing local market conditions. As a responsible landlord, I acknowledge the significance of comprehending the rental market in the areas where my properties are situated. Conducting comprehensive research and keeping oneself updated on the latest trends and data permits informed decision-making when it comes to rent increases.

To gain insights into the local rental market, I scrutinize vacancy rates, rental prices of comparable properties, and any recent changes in supply and demand. This research aids in evaluating whether the proposed rent increase aligns with the current market conditions. It is essential to avoid implementing excessive rent increases that are inconsistent with the rental market, as this could result in housing instability and potential financial hardships for my tenants.

Providing ample notice is another ethical aspect that necessitates consideration when implementing rent increases. Transparency and open communication are crucial for maintaining a positive relationship with tenants. I consistently ensure that I provide written notice to my tenants well in advance of the proposed rent increase, allowing them sufficient time to adjust their budgets and plan accordingly.

The issue of providing notice for a rent increase requires a delicate and sensitive approach. I approach it empathetically and with sensitivity, understanding that my tenants may have concerns or questions. I make myself readily available to address any inquiries they may have and offer clear and detailed explanations regarding the reasons for the increase. This open dialogue facilitates trust and understanding, ensuring that both parties are aligned and can work towards a mutually beneficial resolution.

Furthermore, as an ethical landlord, I acknowledge that some tenants may encounter financial challenges that make it challenging for them to accommodate a sudden increase in rent. In such cases, I am willing to explore alternative solutions that can alleviate their financial strain. This may involve establishing a payment plan, temporarily scaling back the increase, or, in some instances, even freezing the rent to provide stability and support to those in need.

Implementing rent increases responsibly entails a thoughtful and personalized approach rather than a one-size-fits-all solution. It necessitates careful consideration of tenant affordability, local market conditions, and providing adequate notice. By taking these factors into account, my aim is to strike a balance between maintaining a sustainable rental business and safeguarding the well-being of my tenants.

As an ethical landlord, implementing rent increases responsibly holds utmost significance to me. By considering factors such as tenant affordability, local market conditions, and ensuring sufficient notice, I strive to ensure that the rent increases are just and reasonable. This approach is not only ethically correct, but it also fosters positive relationships with my tenants, ultimately creating a harmonious and mutually beneficial environment for both parties involved.

Supporting Renters' Rights and Advocacy

As a landlord committed to upholding ethical standards, I firmly believe in the importance of respecting renters' rights and advocating for fair housing policies. It is not only my ethical obligation, but also a responsibility inherent in the role of being a landlord. Throughout my experience, I have observed the challenges faced by tenants and recognize the imperative of amplifying their voices.

Renters' rights are foundational in ensuring that tenants can reside in secure, comfortable, and equitable conditions. It is essential for landlords to familiarize themselves with these rights and effectively communicate them to their tenants. By doing so, we can establish a transparent and respectful relationship with tenants that fosters trust and understanding.

Encouraging the formation of tenant associations is a key strategy to support renters' rights. These associations serve as collective bodies formed by tenants to address common issues and advocate for their rights. By acknowledging and respecting tenant associations, landlords can facilitate meaningful dialogue and work towards mutually beneficial resolutions.

Legal resources also play a vital role in empowering tenants and guaranteeing the protection of their rights. Landlords should proactively inform their tenants about available legal resources, such as tenant rights organizations, legal aid clinics, and pro bono legal services. Renters must be knowledgeable about their rights and comprehend the legal avenues they can pursue if their rights are violated. As an ethical landlord, I make a point of providing my tenants with information on tenant rights and access to legal assistance, ensuring they possess the necessary resources to protect their interests.

Community initiatives are equally crucial in advocating for fair housing policies and supporting renters' rights. Landlords should actively engage in local community programs, organizations, and initiatives that aim to address housing issues. By collaborating with tenant advocacy groups, housing nonprofits, and government agencies, we can collectively work towards improving housing conditions, strengthening tenants' rights, and promoting fairness in the rental market.

Besides supporting tenant associations and providing legal resources, landlords can adopt proactive measures to safeguard renters' rights. Regular property maintenance and timely resolution of repair issues are essential in guaranteeing that tenants have habitable living environments. Additionally, landlords can implement fair and transparent rental policies, such as reasonable rent increases, clear lease agreements, and equitable screening processes.

By emphasizing the importance of supporting renters' rights and advocating for fair housing policies, landlords can contribute to a more equitable and just rental market. It is crucial for landlords to recognize that tenants are not mere sources of profit, but individuals with rights that warrant protection and respect. By actively participating in the dialogue surrounding renters' rights and being open to feedback and suggestions from tenants, landlords can foster a positive and inclusive living environment for all.

From a personal standpoint, I firmly believe that ethical landlords have a significant role to play in shaping the rental landscape and ensuring fairness and justice for tenants. As an ethical landlord myself, I continually strive to create an environment where my tenants feel safe, respected, and supported. I actively seek partnerships with local tenant advocacy organizations, attend workshops and conferences on fair housing policies, and engage with my tenants to understand their concerns and needs.

Through these experiences, I have come to comprehend the immense importance of supporting renters' rights and advocating for fair housing policies. Merely adhering to legal requirements when renting out a property falls short; we must go beyond that and actively work towards generating a positive and equitable rental experience for all tenants.

Supporting renters' rights and advocating for fair housing policies is an indispensable responsibility that ethical landlords cannot ignore. By highlighting the significance of tenant associations, legal resources, and community initiatives, we can create a rental market that prioritizes fairness, transparency, and respect. As ethical landlords, we possess the power to make a positive impact on the lives of our tenants and contribute to a society where everyone has access to safe, affordable, and dignified housing.

Addressing Income Disparities and Affordable Housing

The presence of unequal incomes and the lack of affordable housing present significant obstacles to many individuals and communities. As a responsible and principled landlord, it is imperative to proactively seek resolutions for these challenges. This chapter will explore a range of approaches that can be employed to effectively tackle income disparities and promote the availability of affordable housing.

1. Rent Subsidy Programs:

Rent subsidy programs play a pivotal role in ensuring that individuals and families with lower incomes have the ability to access affordable housing. By offering financial assistance to tenants, these programs enable them to afford rental properties that would otherwise be unattainable. As an ethical landlord, I am dedicated to supporting rent subsidy programs and fostering collaboration with government agencies and nonprofit organizations that administer them.

Participating effectively in rent subsidy programs requires an in-depth understanding of their complexities. It is crucial to conduct thorough research and remain up-to-date on the specific requirements, benefits, and limitations of these programs. By being well-informed, landlords can guarantee the provision of accurate information to potential tenants and facilitate a seamless application process.

Moreover, an ethical landlord must ensure that the rental properties they offer meet the high standards prescribed by rent subsidy programs. Regular inspections, maintenance, and prompt resolution of issues are crucial elements in fostering positive relationships with both tenants and program administrators.

2. Income-Based Rent Calculation:

Income-based rent calculations represent another ethical approach to addressing income disparities and promoting the availability of affordable housing. Instead of charging a fixed rental amount, this method determines rent based on the tenant's income. By doing so, it ensures that individuals with lower incomes contribute a fair portion of their earnings towards housing, while also allowing landlords to cover their expenses.

Implementing income-based rent calculations requires a transparent and collaborative approach. It is important to establish a clear process for verifying income, such as requesting pay stubs or tax returns, and regularly reassessing rent based on changes in tenants' income. Openly communicating the rationale behind income-based rent calculations is also essential, as it enhances tenants' understanding and appreciation of the fairness of this approach.

Additionally, an ethical landlord should demonstrate consideration for potential fluctuations in tenants' income and strive to create a supportive environment. Offering flexible lease terms, providing resources for job training and educational opportunities, and fostering a sense of community within the rental properties can all contribute to the overall success and well-being of tenants.

3. Partnerships with Affordable Housing Organizations:

Collaborating with affordable housing organizations offers another ethical avenue for addressing income disparities and promoting access to affordable housing. These organizations specialize in developing, managing, and advocating for affordable housing initiatives. Establishing partnerships with such organizations can be mutually beneficial, as they provide valuable expertise and resources while affording landlords the opportunity to make meaningful contributions to their community.

Forging partnerships with affordable housing organizations necessitates the establishment of trust, open communication, and shared objectives. Participating in joint initiatives and projects enables landlords to actively contribute to expanding the availability of affordable housing within their community. This includes considering the development of new affordable housing units or converting existing properties into affordable rentals.

Furthermore, partnering with affordable housing organizations provides access to additional support services for tenants, such as financial literacy programs, counseling, or employment assistance. The comprehensive approach embraced by these organizations ensures that individuals not only have access to affordable housing but are also equipped with the tools and resources necessary for long-term stability and success.

Conclusion:

Addressing income disparities and promoting access to affordable housing demands a multifaceted and ethical approach. Rent subsidy programs, income-based rent calculations, and partnerships with affordable housing organizations are just a few of the many strategies that can be employed. As a responsible landlord, I am deeply committed to actively engaging in these efforts and continually seeking new opportunities to positively impact the housing needs of individuals and communities. By working collaboratively towards a more equitable and affordable future, we can create a society where everyone, regardless of income, has access to safe and affordable housing.

Legal Considerations in Ethical Rent Pricing

As an ethical landlord, it is crucial to be well-versed in the relevant laws, regulations, and guidelines pertaining to rent pricing, tenant rights, and fair housing practices. Operating within the bounds of the law not only safeguards you from potential legal consequences but also reinforces your commitment to upholding ethical standards and protecting the rights of your tenants.

Rent Control Laws: In certain jurisdictions, rent control laws are in place to regulate the amount by which landlords can increase rent prices. These laws aim to promote housing affordability and prevent excessive rent hikes that could displace tenants. As a responsible landlord, familiarizing yourself with local rent control ordinances is essential to ensure compliance and avoid any legal repercussions.

Notice Requirements: Many states and municipalities have specific notice requirements that landlords must adhere to when increasing rent prices. These laws stipulate the minimum amount of written notice, typically ranging from 30 to 90 days, that must be provided to tenants before a rent increase can take effect. Failure to comply with these notice requirements could result in legal disputes or penalties.

Tenant Rights and Protections: It is imperative to have a comprehensive understanding of tenant rights and protections established by state and local laws. These protections cover various aspects, such as the right to habitable living conditions, freedom from discrimination, and the right to privacy. Violating tenant rights could expose you to legal liabilities and undermine your ethical standing as a landlord.

Fair Housing Laws: Fair housing laws prohibit discrimination in housing practices based on protected characteristics such as race, color, religion, national origin, sex, familial status, and disability. As an ethical landlord, you must ensure that your rent pricing strategies, tenant screening processes, and overall rental practices comply with fair housing laws. Violations of these laws can result in severe legal consequences, including fines and potential lawsuits.

Lease Agreement Provisions: The lease agreement is a legally binding contract between you and your tenants. It is essential to carefully review and understand the provisions related to rent pricing, rent increases, and any associated fees or charges. Ensuring that your lease agreements are clear, transparent, and in compliance with applicable laws will help mitigate potential legal disputes and protect the rights of both parties.

State and Local Landlord-Tenant Laws: Each state and locality may have specific landlord-tenant laws that govern various aspects of the rental process, including rent pricing, security deposits, eviction procedures, and more. Familiarizing yourself with these laws is crucial to ensure that your rental practices align with legal requirements and avoid any potential violations.

By staying informed and compliant with relevant laws, regulations, and guidelines, you can navigate the legal landscape surrounding rent pricing, tenant rights, and fair housing practices with confidence. Additionally, it is advisable to consult with legal professionals or housing organizations when faced with complex legal matters or ambiguities, as they can provide valuable guidance and ensure that you remain on the right side of the law while upholding your ethical principles as a landlord.

Striking the Balance: Ethics and Profitability in Rent Pricing

As ethical landlords, we are tasked with the delicate responsibility of balancing our moral obligation to implement fair and equitable rent pricing practices with the practical need to maintain a financially sustainable business model. This balance is a crucial aspect of ethical landlordship, as it ensures the long-term viability of our endeavors while upholding the principles of transparency, affordability, and tenant well-being.

At the core of this balance lies the recognition that profit should not be the sole driving force behind our rent pricing decisions. While generating a reasonable return on investment is necessary to sustain and grow our rental business, it should never come at the expense of exploiting or overburdening our tenants. Ethical rent pricing requires a holistic approach that considers not only our financial goals but also the socioeconomic realities of the communities we serve.

One effective strategy to achieve this balance is to conduct comprehensive market research and cost analysis. By thoroughly understanding the local rental market trends, comparable property prices, and our operational expenses, we can establish rent prices that are competitive, fair, and aligned with the affordability levels of our target tenant demographic. This data-driven approach ensures that our rent prices are grounded in economic realities rather than arbitrary or exploitative figures.

Additionally, we must be willing to explore alternative revenue streams and cost-saving measures that can supplement our income without placing an undue burden on our tenants. This could involve leveraging ancillary services, implementing energy-efficient upgrades to reduce utility costs, or exploring partnerships with local businesses or organizations that align with our ethical values.

Fostering open communication with our tenants is another crucial aspect of maintaining this balance. By actively seeking feedback and engaging in transparent dialogues, we can gain valuable insights into our tenants' financial situations and housing needs. This information can then inform our rent pricing strategies, allowing us to make informed decisions that prioritize affordability while still generating sustainable revenue.

Furthermore, we must be proactive in exploring and leveraging government incentives, subsidies, or tax credits designed to support affordable housing initiatives. By aligning our rental business with these programs, we can access valuable resources that can help offset potential revenue gaps resulting from implementing ethical rent pricing practices.

It is also essential to adopt a long-term perspective when balancing ethics and profitability in rent pricing. While implementing ethical practices may result in short-term financial trade-offs, the benefits of cultivating a positive reputation, fostering tenant loyalty, and contributing to a stable and thriving community can yield dividends in the form of sustained occupancy rates, reduced turnover costs, and increased property values over time.

Ultimately, striking the right balance between ethics and profitability in rent pricing requires a mindset shift – one that recognizes the intrinsic value of ethical business practices and their ability to drive long-term success. By prioritizing transparency, affordability, and tenant well-being, we not only uphold our moral principles but also create a virtuous cycle that attracts responsible tenants, fosters positive community relations, and establishes a solid foundation for sustainable business growth.

While navigating this balance may present challenges and require ongoing adjustments, embracing ethical rent pricing practices is not only the right thing to do but also a strategic investment in the future of our rental business and the communities we serve.

Chapter 4: Legal and Ethical Responsibilities of Landlords

Understanding Landlord-Tenant Laws

As a responsible and ethical landlord, it is crucial to possess a thorough comprehension of the various laws and regulations governing the landlord-tenant relationship. These laws not only safeguard the rights of both parties but also establish equity and prevent any instances of discrimination or exploitation. This chapter will explore the key elements of landlord-tenant laws, encompassing lease agreements, security deposits, eviction procedures, and anti-discrimination laws.

1. Lease agreements:

An essential component of the landlord-tenant relationship is the lease agreement, which forms a legally binding document outlining the terms and conditions governing the rental arrangement. Familiarizing oneself with the specific requirements and provisions that must be included in a lease agreement is imperative for landlords, as these can vary based on jurisdiction.

A well-crafted lease agreement should clearly delineate the rights and responsibilities of both the landlord and the tenant. It should encompass crucial aspects such as the duration of the tenancy, rent payment terms, maintenance obligations, and any applicable restrictions or regulations tenants must adhere to. Additionally, it is crucial to incorporate provisions regarding rent escalation, late payment penalties, and lease termination procedures.

Through ensuring comprehensiveness and clarity in the lease agreement, landlords can minimize the occurrence of conflicts or misunderstandings with tenants. Moreover, possessing a robust understanding of the laws concerning lease agreements will enable landlords to adhere to legal prerequisites and avert potential liability concerns.

2. Security deposits:

Security deposits serve as a means of protecting landlords against potential damages caused by tenants during their occupancy. However, the handling of security deposits is bound by specific laws and regulations aimed at safeguarding tenants' rights and preventing arbitrary deductions.

Comprehending the legal requirements surrounding security deposits is vital for landlords, including the maximum allowable amount that can be charged and the timeframe within which they must be returned. In many jurisdictions, landlords are obligated to hold security deposits in a separate account, known as a trust account, to prevent the mingling of funds.

Furthermore, landlords are required to furnish tenants with a written statement elucidating any deductions made from their security deposit, along with the reasons for those deductions. Failure to conform to these legal obligations may result in penalties and potential legal ramifications.

3. Eviction processes:

While eviction should be considered a last resort, landlords must be well-versed in the legal procedures and requirements should such a circumstance arise. Eviction laws differ between jurisdictions, therefore, understanding the specific regulations applicable to one's location is crucial.

Before initiating an eviction, landlords must ensure that they possess valid justifications, such as non-payment of rent, lease term violations, or illegal activities. It is essential to provide tenants with proper notice, adhering to the prescribed timeframes and methods stipulated by law. Landlords must also understand the documentation and evidence required to support a legitimate eviction case, as well as the requisite court procedures to follow.

Furthermore, it is essential to operate within legal boundaries and refrain from taking matters into one's own hands, even when faced with difficult or non-compliant tenants. Engaging the services of legal professionals and cooperating closely with the court system ensures that the eviction process remains fair, legal, and immune to potential legal repercussions.

4. Anti-discrimination laws:

For landlords, strict adherence to anti-discrimination laws in all facets of renting, encompassing tenant selection, lease renewal, and termination, is of utmost importance. These laws prohibit landlords from engaging in discriminatory practices against tenants based on protected characteristics such as race, color, religion, national origin, sex, disability, familial status, or any other legally protected status.

Comprehending the anti-discrimination laws applicable in one's jurisdiction is pivotal for landlords to ensure that they conduct their business in a fair and lawful manner. This includes familiarizing oneself with guidelines pertaining to fair housing advertisements, conducting tenant screenings in a non-discriminatory manner, and treating all applicants and tenants with fairness and respect.

By upholding anti-discrimination laws, landlords actively contribute to the establishment of inclusive and harmonious communities, foster trusting relationships with tenants, and preserve their own reputation.

Possessing a comprehensive understanding of landlord-tenant laws is indispensable for any ethical landlord. By providing an overview of lease agreements, security deposits, eviction procedures, and anti-discrimination laws, this chapter has served as an invaluable guide to assist landlords in complying with legal obligations and maintaining a fair and ethical landlord-tenant relationship.

Ethical Tenant Screening Practices

The process of screening prospective tenants is a critical component of responsible property management. However, it is essential to ensure that this process is conducted in an ethical and non-discriminatory manner, free from biases or discriminatory practices that could potentially violate fair housing laws and infringe upon the rights of applicants.

As a first step, landlords should establish clear and objective screening criteria that are consistently applied to all applicants. These criteria should be based on legitimate considerations such as creditworthiness, employment history, and rental history, without regard to protected characteristics such as race, color, religion, national origin, sex, disability, or familial status.

To mitigate the risk of unconscious biases influencing the screening process, landlords can implement standardized application forms and scoring systems. These tools help ensure that all applicants are evaluated based on the same set of objective criteria, reducing the potential for subjective judgments that could lead to discrimination.

Furthermore, it is crucial to maintain strict confidentiality and privacy protocols when handling applicant information. Any personal or sensitive data collected during the screening process should be treated with the utmost care and used solely for the purposes of evaluating the applicant's qualifications. Landlords should also be transparent about the types of information being collected and the reasons for doing so.

In cases where landlords rely on third-party screening services or background check providers, it is important to carefully vet these companies to ensure that their practices are compliant with fair housing laws and do not engage in discriminatory practices. Landlords should also review the reports provided by these services to ensure that the information is accurate and relevant to the screening criteria.

Addressing Potential Biases and Discrimination

Despite best efforts, unconscious biases can still creep into the screening process. To address this, landlords should implement regular training and awareness programs for themselves and their staff. These programs should focus on recognizing and mitigating implicit biases, as well as providing education on fair housing laws and best practices for non-discriminatory screening.

Additionally, landlords should establish clear procedures for handling complaints or concerns related to potential discrimination. These procedures should include a fair and impartial investigation process, as well as appropriate remedial actions if discrimination is found to have occurred.

It is also important to regularly review screening practices and outcomes to identify any potential disparities or patterns that may indicate the presence of biases or discrimination. This can involve analyzing data on applicant demographics, approval rates, and reasons for denial, and making necessary adjustments to address any identified issues.

By implementing ethical tenant screening practices and actively addressing potential biases and discrimination, landlords can not only comply with fair housing laws but also foster an environment of inclusivity and equal opportunity. This not only benefits prospective tenants but also contributes to the creation of diverse and vibrant communities within rental properties.

Maintaining Property Safety and Security

As a landlord, I have always believed that my responsibilities extend well beyond the mere collection of rent. While it is true that providing a safe and secure living environment benefits both the tenants and myself, there is an ethical obligation that I have fully embraced. In this chapter, we will explore the various aspects of maintaining property safety and security, including the importance of proper maintenance, fire safety measures, and protecting tenant privacy. By comprehending and fulfilling these obligations, landlords can establish an environment that not only meets legal requirements but also nurtures trust and peace of mind for their tenants.

Proper Maintenance:

One of the primary obligations of a landlord is to ensure that the property is well-maintained. From an ethical standpoint, this entails conducting regular inspections and promptly addressing any issues that may compromise the safety or comfort of the tenants. Whether it involves a leaking pipe, a faulty electrical outlet, or a loose stair railing, these matters cannot be disregarded.

Proper maintenance not only preserves the property's condition but also prevents accidents and potential injuries. By promptly addressing maintenance needs, landlords can cultivate trust and reliability among their tenants. Regular inspections allow me to proactively identify any potential hazards and take necessary steps to rectify them. From an ethical perspective, this is essential, as it demonstrates my dedication to the well-being of those who reside in my properties.

Fire Safety:

Fire safety is a crucial aspect of maintaining property safety and security. Fires can cause devastating damage and pose significant risks to human life. As a responsible landlord, I prioritize fire safety measures in my properties to safeguard the lives and belongings of my tenants.

This begins with the installation and regular maintenance of smoke detectors in every unit. Smoke detectors provide early warnings that enable tenants to evacuate the premises in the event of a fire. I make it a priority to regularly test these detectors and replace the batteries as necessary. Additionally, I ensure that fire extinguishers are strategically placed throughout the property, easily accessible to all tenants.

Furthermore, I collaborate with local fire departments to conduct fire safety drills and educate tenants on emergency procedures. By investing time and resources into fire safety, I am not only fulfilling my ethical obligation but also demonstrating to my tenants that their well-being is of the utmost importance to me.

Protecting Tenant Privacy:

Respecting and safeguarding tenant privacy is an ethical duty that should not be disregarded. As landlords, we have access to sensitive information about our tenants, including personal and financial details. It is our responsibility to handle this information with the utmost care and respect their privacy rights.

To uphold tenant privacy, I take several measures. Firstly, I restrict access to tenant information to only authorized personnel within my property management team. I ensure that this information is securely stored and solely utilized for legitimate and necessary purposes.

Second, I honor the boundaries and privacy of my tenants in their daily lives. I provide them notice before entering their units for inspections or repairs, unless there is an emergency situation. This courtesy allows tenants to feel secure and respected in their own homes.

In this digital age, the ethical duty of protecting tenant privacy also extends to online platforms. I ensure that any online rental applications or payment systems provided by my management company are secure and safeguard the sensitive information of my tenants from unauthorized access.

Maintaining property safety and security is an ethical obligation that surpasses legal requirements. As landlords, we must go above and beyond to ensure the well-being and peace of mind of our tenants. Proper maintenance, fire safety measures, and protecting tenant privacy are all essential aspects of this duty.

By fulfilling these obligations in an ethical manner, landlords nurture trust and create an environment where tenants feel safe and secure. It is not solely about fulfilling legal requirements; it is about establishing a home where tenants can genuinely feel comfortable. As the ethical duty of a landlord, maintaining property safety and security should always be a top priority.

Ethical Handling of Tenant Privacy and Personal Information

As a responsible landlord, I prioritize the respect of my tenants' privacy rights. This involves acknowledging and abiding by their established boundaries, as well as preserving the confidentiality of their personal information. I strictly adhere to procedures and protocols within my operations to ensure the secure handling of personal information. Any personal information provided by tenants, whether through application forms or during their tenancy, is securely and confidentially stored. I have invested in state-of-the-art data management systems that incorporate comprehensive security measures to safeguard tenant information. These measures include encrypted databases, firewalls, and regular security audits to promptly address any vulnerabilities.

To maintain compliance with data protection regulations, myself and my staff are well-informed on relevant legislation, such as the General Data Protection Regulation (GDPR) in Europe or the California Consumer Privacy Act (CCPA) in the United States. Staying updated on changes and updates to these regulations is critical to ensure compliance and maintain trust with tenants.

To demonstrate my commitment to tenant privacy, I have implemented transparency measures. This includes providing tenants with clear information regarding the use, access, and retention period of their personal data. Such transparency fosters trust between myself and my tenants, assuring them that their personal information is handled responsibly and in their best interest.

Obtaining informed consent is crucial to ethically handling tenant privacy. Prior to collecting any personal information, tenants are fully informed about the purpose for which it will be used and whether any third parties will have access to it. This empowers tenants to make an informed decision regarding the provision of certain information, upholding the integrity of the landlord-tenant relationship.

In addition to respect for tenant privacy, it is essential to establish a clear process for responsible handling of tenant personal information. This involves adhering to the principle of data minimization, collecting and storing only the necessary and relevant information. By limiting the amount of data collected, the risk of unauthorized access or breaches is minimized, enhancing the overall security of tenant personal information.

Within my organization, stringent access controls are in place to further protect tenant privacy. Only authorized personnel with legitimate reasons for accessing tenant information are granted permission. Regular training and awareness programs ensure that employees understand the importance of maintaining the confidentiality of personal information and the potential consequences of data breaches.

Openness and transparency are imperative in the event of any data breaches or incidents. Should a breach occur, prompt action is taken to mitigate potential harm to tenants, and they are promptly and transparently informed. This allows tenants to take necessary precautions to protect themselves, such as monitoring their accounts or changing passwords.

In conclusion, the ethical handling of tenant privacy and personal information is a paramount concern for responsible landlords. Upholding tenants' privacy rights, responsibly managing personal information, and complying with data protection regulations form the core principles of ethical practice in this field. By proactively implementing measures to safeguard tenant privacy, landlords can cultivate trust with their tenants and establish a safe and secure environment for all parties involved.

Ethical Approaches to Tenant Evictions

In order to carry out tenant evictions in a professional and ethical manner, it is of utmost importance to ensure that sufficient notice is provided. This allows tenants ample time to address any issues or problems that have led to the eviction process, giving them the opportunity to rectify their situation or make alternative arrangements in order to potentially avoid eviction altogether.

In my experience, effective and clear communication is a key element when it comes to giving notice to tenants. To maintain transparency and ensure that both parties have a comprehensive understanding of the situation at hand, all communication is conducted in written form, whether through letters or emails, in order to establish a paper trail. Furthermore, I place great emphasis on providing detailed notices that clearly outline the reasons for eviction and any necessary steps that the tenant can take to rectify the situation. This approach serves to protect my interests as a landlord and foster transparency and fairness throughout the eviction process.

When considering alternative solutions, I strongly believe in exploring every available option to avoid eviction. This includes engaging in open and honest conversations with tenants in order to identify the root causes of their difficulties and finding ways to address them that do not involve eviction. For instance, I may offer flexible payment plans to tenants who are struggling with meeting their rent obligations or connect them with local community resources for financial assistance. Moreover, I am open to considering other housing options that may better suit their needs.

The aim of these alternative solutions is to demonstrate compassion and empathy towards tenants instead of resorting to eviction as the initial and sole solution. By doing so, I am able to minimize the adverse impacts on the tenant's life that may arise from eviction, such as homelessness or other negative consequences.

Minimizing the undue hardships faced by tenants is an integral aspect of ethical tenant evictions. Recognizing the potential disruptions that evictions can bring about in a tenant's life, including the risk of homelessness, it is crucial to approach the eviction process with empathy and genuine concern for the well-being of the tenant.

In order to minimize these hardships, I place great emphasis on providing support and resources to tenants throughout the eviction process. This entails ensuring that tenants are well-informed about their rights and entitlements, including any available housing assistance programs or organizations that may be able to provide them with temporary shelter or financial support during this challenging time. By assisting tenants in navigating the eviction process and offering resources, I strive to mitigate the negative impact on their lives as much as possible.

Furthermore, I believe in the importance of fairness and reasonableness when it comes to enforcing eviction orders. If a tenant is actively working towards resolving their issues or making efforts to comply with the terms of their lease, I may consider granting them additional time or reevaluating their situation to explore further alternative solutions. This approach allows me to strike a balance between protecting my property and fulfilling my commitment to assisting tenants in difficult circumstances.

Adopting ethical approaches to tenant evictions involves providing sufficient notice, offering alternative solutions, and minimizing undue hardships. As an ethical landlord, I strive to balance the need to protect my property and maintain the integrity of my role with a genuine commitment to demonstrating empathy and compassion towards tenants facing eviction. Through adhering to these ethical considerations, I believe we can create a rental market that is more compassionate and fair, benefiting both landlords and tenants alike.

Ethical Treatment of Special Tenant Groups

One of the foremost and indispensable steps in ethically addressing special tenant groups is to possess a thorough comprehension of the laws and regulations pertaining to their rights. In many nations, including my own, there exists legislatively mandated protection against discriminatory practices targeting individuals with disabilities, and guarantees their entitlement to equitable access to housing. These legal provisions mandate landlords to make appropriate adjustments for tenants with disabilities, thereby ensuring that they are afforded identical opportunities to enjoy their living arrangements as any other tenant.

Reasonable accommodations can take various forms, contingent upon the unique needs of the individual. For instance, a tenant with mobility impairments may necessitate the installation of ramps or handrails to gain entry to their apartment, while a visually impaired tenant may require braille signage or auditory assistance within the building. As an ethical landlord, it is incumbent upon me to assess these needs on a case-by-case basis, and to implement measures that guarantee equal access and comfort for all tenants.

Accessibility extends beyond physical accommodations and encompasses addressing the distinctive requirements of elderly tenants. As individuals age, they may necessitate certain modifications to their living spaces to ensure their safety and well-being. Such alterations could involve the installation of grab bars in bathrooms, the adjustment of countertops and shelves for enhanced accessibility, or the provision of adequate lighting throughout the premises. By preemptively considering the needs of elderly tenants, I am not only fulfilling my ethical obligations, but also cultivating an environment that facilitates independence and longevity for such individuals.

Another special tenant group necessitating ethical consideration is families with children. It is imperative for landlords to furnish a safe and nurturing environment for these families, given that children are particularly vulnerable and rely on the adults around them for support. This can be accomplished through the elimination of hazards within the property, such as lead-based paint or faulty electrical wiring, as well as by cultivating a positive and inclusive community atmosphere.

Moreover, landlords ought to be cognizant of the potential impact their actions may engender upon families with children during the eviction process. Whilst it may be occasionally necessary to evict tenants who are unable to fulfill their obligations, tact and empathy must be exercised to minimize any disruptions experienced by families, particularly during the academic year. By demonstrating empathy and providing support during times of transition, I can foster a sense of stability and well-being for these families.

In addition to fulfilling legal obligations, there also exists moral and ethical responsibilities that, in my opinion, every landlord should uphold. My philosophy is rooted in empathy, compassion, and an unwavering belief in equality of opportunity for all. To me, being a landlord means that I am not solely an owner of properties, but also a guardian of people's homes and well-being.

In order to ensure that special tenant groups are treated in an ethical manner, I have implemented various initiatives within my properties. Firstly, I have established an open channel of communication with tenants, encouraging them to share any concerns or specific needs they may have. This ongoing dialogue enables me to gain a better understanding of their individual circumstances, and aids in identifying areas where enhancements can be made.

Moreover, I have made a commitment to conduct regular inspections of my properties. These inspections are not only intended to identify any maintenance or safety issues, but also to ascertain that the adaptations and accommodations provided are functioning as intended. This proactive approach empowers me to promptly address any issues that may arise, thereby minimizing inconveniences experienced by my tenants and guaranteeing their safety and well-being.

Additionally, I have placed great emphasis on the training of my property management staff, ensuring that they possess a comprehensive understanding of the rights and needs of special tenant groups. This equips them to provide knowledgeable assistance and support to tenants with disabilities, elderly tenants, and families with children. I firmly believe that investing in education and professional development is crucial in forging a culture that prioritizes ethical and inclusive housing practices.

Lastly, as part of my commitment to the ethical treatment of special tenant groups, I have fostered a sense of community within my properties. This community promotes diversity, inclusivity, and mutual respect. By nurturing positive relationships amongst tenants, regardless of their differences, my aim is to create an environment where each individual feels valued and supported.

Treating special tenant groups in an ethical manner necessitates a combination of adhering to legal requirements, embracing moral responsibilities, and adopting proactive measures. As an ethical landlord, I acknowledge the significance of providing reasonable accommodations and ensuring accessibility for individuals with disabilities, elderly tenants, and families with children. By understanding their distinct requirements and implementing measures to address them, I am capable of creating an environment that fosters equality, well-being, and community within my properties.

Building a Positive and Inclusive Community

Cultivating a positive and inclusive community within rental properties can significantly enhance the overall experience for tenants. A strong sense of community not only fosters a harmonious living environment but also instills a sense of belonging and security for residents. As a responsible landlord, it is crucial to recognize the importance of nurturing a community-oriented atmosphere and to actively implement strategies that promote inclusivity and mutual respect among tenants.

One effective approach to building a positive community is to facilitate opportunities for social interaction and engagement. This can be achieved through the organization of regular community events, such as potluck gatherings, outdoor activities, or even book clubs. By creating a platform for tenants to interact and connect with one another, a sense of camaraderie and familiarity can develop, fostering a more cohesive and supportive community.

It is also essential to establish clear guidelines and expectations for respectful behavior within the community. This can be achieved through the implementation of a community code of conduct, which outlines the standards for interaction and emphasizes the importance of treating all tenants with dignity and respect, regardless of their backgrounds or personal circumstances. By setting these expectations from the outset, a foundation of mutual understanding and consideration is established.

Additionally, landlords can play a pivotal role in promoting inclusivity by actively embracing diversity within their rental communities. This involves creating an environment where tenants of all ages, races, ethnicities, religions, and abilities feel welcomed and valued. Celebrating and acknowledging cultural differences through events or displays can foster a greater appreciation for diversity and contribute to a more harmonious community.

Effective communication is another critical component in building a positive community. Establishing open lines of communication between landlords, property managers, and tenants can help address any concerns or issues promptly and transparently. Regular community meetings or newsletters can serve as platforms for sharing updates, addressing common concerns, and gathering feedback from tenants.

Furthermore, landlords can enhance the sense of community by providing shared spaces and amenities that encourage social interaction. These may include community rooms, outdoor recreational areas, or even community gardens, where tenants can come together, socialize, and engage in activities that foster a sense of belonging.

By prioritizing the development of a positive and inclusive community, landlords can create an environment where tenants feel valued, respected, and secure. A strong community can also contribute to increased tenant satisfaction and retention, as individuals are more likely to remain in a living environment where they feel a sense of belonging and support.

In conclusion, building a positive and inclusive community within rental properties requires a multifaceted approach that involves fostering social interaction, establishing clear guidelines for respectful behavior, embracing diversity, maintaining open communication, and providing shared spaces and amenities. By implementing these strategies, landlords can significantly enhance the overall tenant experience, creating a harmonious and supportive living environment that benefits both residents and property owners alike.

Chapter 5: Sustainable and Ethical Property Management

Energy Efficiency and Conservation

As a landlord committed to ethical practices, it is incumbent upon me to ensure that my properties not only provide comfortable living spaces for tenants, but also contribute to a sustainable future. Energy efficiency and conservation play a pivotal role in achieving this objective. Within this chapter, I will explore the significance of energy-efficient property management, encompassing sustainable building practices, energy audits, and the promotion of tenant energy conservation.

Sustainable Building Practices:

One of the core areas in which I prioritize energy efficiency is the construction and refurbishment of my rental properties. Sustainable building practices not only diminish the carbon footprint of the building but also result in long-term savings in energy expenses. To accomplish this, I collaborate with environmentally-conscious architects and contractors who incorporate energy-efficient features into the design and construction processes.

These features may entail enhanced insulation, energy-efficient windows and doors, solar panels, and even geothermal heating and cooling systems. By integrating these elements, I am able to significantly reduce energy consumption, which benefits both the environment and the financial bottom line. Moreover, these features render my properties more appealing to tenants who value environmental sustainability, allowing me to sustain high occupancy rates.

Energy Audits:

To evaluate the energy consumption and identify areas for improvement in my properties, I regularly conduct energy audits. These audits involve a comprehensive evaluation of the building systems and appliances to identify where energy efficiency can be enhanced. I engage certified energy auditors who employ advanced diagnostic tools to assess the performance of the properties and offer actionable recommendations.

During an energy audit, auditors inspect insulation levels, air leakage, heating and cooling systems, lighting, and appliances. This meticulous analysis assists me in understanding where energy is being wasted and how I can make cost-effective improvements. For instance, if the audit reveals inadequate insulation in the attic, I would prioritize upgrading the insulation to minimize heat loss during the winter and reduce cooling needs during the summer.

Promoting Tenant Energy Conservation:

While sustainable building practices and energy audits optimize energy efficiency at the property level, it is equally important to foster a culture of energy conservation among tenants. Empowering tenants to be mindful of their energy consumption not only reduces environmental impact, but also mitigates their utility bills.

Educating tenants on energy-saving practices is one way to promote tenant energy conservation. I furnish them with informational packets or organize informational sessions to acquaint them with simple actions they can take to reduce energy consumption. These actions may include switching off lights upon exiting a room, utilizing energy-efficient light bulbs, adjusting thermostats to conserve energy, and properly maintaining appliances.

I also encourage tenants to avail themselves of governmental programs and incentives that aim to promote energy efficiency. This could involve programs that provide energy-saving tips and tools, or even financial incentives for adopting energy-efficient appliances or upgrading insulation. By guiding tenants toward these resources, I support their endeavors to conserve energy and reduce their carbon footprint.

In addition to education and awareness, I have implemented incentives to motivate tenants to conserve energy. For instance, I offer a reduced monthly rent to tenants who demonstrate exceptional energy-saving practices. This serves not only as a reward for their efforts, but also fosters a sense of healthy competition among tenants, inspiring them to conserve energy and contribute to a greener environment.

Conclusion:

Energy efficiency and conservation in property management is not solely about cost reduction. It constitutes a crucial aspect of responsible and ethical landlordship. By incorporating sustainable building practices, conducting regular energy audits, and promoting tenant energy conservation, I am not only diminishing the environmental impact of my properties, but also providing a higher value proposition to my tenants.

As an ethical landlord, I recognize it as my duty to champion sustainable living and contribute to a greener future. By implementing energy-efficient property management practices, I am not only fulfilling my moral obligation, but also reaping the benefits of reduced energy expenses and heightened tenant satisfaction. Collectively, we can cultivate a more sustainable and energy-conscious world.

Waste Management and Recycling

One of the primary components of my waste management program entails the implementation of recycling programs. Recycling is a fundamental method for waste reduction and resource conservation, as well as an immensely efficacious means of mitigating the environmental impact of our day-to-day activities. Ensuring convenient and accessible recycling options for tenants remains a significant priority across all my properties. Consequently, designated recycling bins are strategically placed in common areas, while collaborations with local recycling facilities guarantee appropriate processing of the collected materials.

To augment participation in the recycling program, I have taken several measures. Firstly, I have furnished clear guidelines regarding the items suitable for recycling. This endeavor seeks to address misconceptions that frequently result in the contamination of the recycling stream. Furthermore, the placement of conspicuous signage and educational materials in prominent locations, such as near the recycling bins and communal areas, significantly aids tenants in comprehending the significance of proper recycling practices. Additionally, a series of workshops and seminars on recycling, facilitated by experts in the field, have been conducted on a regular basis. These events allow tenants to gain knowledge, pose questions, and voice any concerns they may have. The fostering of community responsibility and increased awareness has yielded a notable increase in recycling participation, thereby leading to a discernible reduction in waste sent to landfills.

Alongside recycling, the adoption of waste reduction strategies comprises an integral facet of my ethical waste management practices. I firmly endorse the notion that prevention supersedes treatment, and thus advocate for measures aimed at diminishing waste generation. By placing considerable emphasis on a conscientious act of consumption, tenants are educated on practices that include the purchase of products with minimal packaging, the utilization of reusable containers and bags, as well as composting.

Of particular significance, composting represents an invaluable waste reduction strategy that not only diverts organic waste from landfills but also contributes to the creation of nutrient-rich soil. Within my properties, composting systems have been implemented, complete with bins for tenants to deposit their food scraps and yard waste. Regular upkeep and emptying of these bins subsequently afford the opportunity to employ the resulting compost to nourish community gardens or provide tenants with personal utilization. By instilling in residents an appreciation for the value of their food waste, along with the means to responsibly dispose of it, we have not only diminished waste production but have also engendered a stronger connection between tenants and the natural environment.

Confronting the responsible disposal of hazardous materials represents yet another critical aspect of ethical waste management. Hazardous materials, including batteries, electronic waste, and chemicals, present pronounced risks to both human health and the environment when mishandled. In light of this, I have implemented stringent guidelines and protocols pertaining to the disposal of such materials within my properties. Tenants are thus afforded a secure and convenient means of eliminating hazardous waste.

To facilitate responsible disposal, designated drop-off points for hazardous materials have been established throughout the properties. These points are equipped with appropriate containment and labeling to deter accidents or leakage. Collaborations with local hazardous waste disposal facilities further allow tenants access to information encompassing the safe and proper elimination of these materials. By addressing this particular aspect of waste management, I not only safeguard the well-being of my tenants but also hold true to my commitment to ethical and sustainable practices.

My ethical approach to waste management as a landlord encompasses comprehensive strategies encompassing recycling programs, waste reduction initiatives, and responsible disposal of hazardous materials. These practices have not only significantly curtailed the environmental impact of my properties but also fostered a sense of community responsibility and awareness among tenants. As ethical landlords, it remains our inherent duty to prioritize sustainable and responsible practices. Through the effective implementation of waste management protocols, we are poised to make substantial contributions toward a cleaner, healthier, and more sustainable future.

Water Conservation and Sustainable Landscaping

Water scarcity is a pressing global issue that necessitates urgent attention. It has been projected that by 2025, a significant portion of the world's population, approximately two-thirds, may encounter water shortages. Hence, it is of utmost importance for landlords to adopt a proactive stance in conserving water within their properties. One effective strategy is the implementation of efficient irrigation systems. Traditional methods, such as sprinklers, often result in excessive water consumption due to evaporation and runoff. By embracing advanced technologies like drip irrigation or smart sprinkler systems, water consumption can be reduced by as much as 50%. These systems facilitate the direct delivery of water to plant roots, thus minimizing waste and ensuring optimal water utilization.

Besides the adoption of efficient irrigation systems, the promotion of native landscaping represents another ethically sound approach to water conservation. Native plants are naturally adapted to local climate conditions and require less water and upkeep compared to non-native species. Incorporating these native plants into our landscaping designs creates habitats better suited to the local ecosystem while simultaneously minimizing the need for excessive watering. Additionally, the use of mulch and compost enhances soil moisture retention, thereby reducing water requirements and fostering healthy plant growth.

It is also our ethical duty as landlords to promote tenant awareness of water-saving practices. Many tenants may not fully comprehend the impact their daily activities can have on water usage. By providing educational resources and consistently engaging with our tenants, we can encourage behaviors that promote water conservation. Simple practices like turning off faucets when not in use, promptly repairing leaky pipes, and utilizing dishwashers and washing machines only when they are fully loaded contribute significantly to water conservation. Furthermore, outdoor activities like car washing and excess lawn watering often lead to considerable water wastage. By working closely with our tenants, we can cultivate responsible water usage habits and impart an understanding of the significance of conservation.

Incentivizing tenants is one approach to cultivate water-saving habits. The implementation of a tiered water pricing system can encourage tenants to be mindful of their water consumption. By charging higher rates for excessive usage and offering rebates for those who conserve water, we establish a system that rewards responsible practices. Additionally, landlords might consider installing water-efficient appliances and fixtures, such as low-flow toilets and faucets, in their properties. Not only does this reduce water consumption, but it also brings about long-term savings on water bills for both tenants and landlords.

To further demonstrate our commitment to ethical water conservation, it is imperative that we regularly assess and improve the water management systems within our properties. Regular audits enable the identification of areas with potential for improvement and gauge the effectiveness of our conservation efforts. This entails evaluating the efficiency of irrigation systems, inspecting for leaks, and monitoring water usage trends. By adopting a proactive approach, we can continually strive to reduce consumption and elevate our conservation practices.

Embracing ethical approaches to water conservation, encompassing efficient irrigation systems, native landscaping, and the promotion of tenant awareness of water-saving practices, constitutes a critical aspect of responsible landlordship. Water is an exhaustible resource, and it is incumbent upon us to ensure its sustainable use within our properties. Proactively conserving water not only lessens our environmental impact but also fosters a healthier living environment for our tenants. Let us continue to prioritize water conservation and sustainable landscaping as we endeavor to become fully responsible landlords.

Ethical Property Upgrades and Renovations

When evaluating property upgrades and renovations, it is crucial to conduct a comprehensive assessment of the project's environmental impact. This entails scrutinizing the materials utilized, the energy efficiency of the new installations, and the waste generated during the construction process. Selecting eco-friendly materials such as recycled or sustainably sourced products, as well as incorporating energy-efficient appliances and fixtures, can significantly diminish the carbon footprint of properties. Furthermore, integrating renewable energy sources such as solar panels or wind turbines can further bolster the property's environmental sustainability.

Tenant comfort must also be a paramount consideration when undertaking property upgrades and renovations. This encompasses factors such as indoor air quality, temperature regulation, and noise reduction. Investing in top-notch ventilation systems, insulation, and soundproofing materials can create a comfortable and healthy living environment for tenants. Additionally, integrating smart home technology like programmable thermostats or automated lighting systems can enhance tenant comfort while concurrently reducing energy consumption and utility costs.

Preserving the historical or cultural significance of a property is an additional aspect that should not be disregarded. Many structures hold stories and memories that are deeply intertwined with the local community's history. By maintaining and restoring historical features, landlords can contribute to safeguarding the distinctive character and identity of a location. This might entail upholding original architecture, refurbishing antique fixtures, or even commissioning local artists to create murals or sculptures that reflect the property's history. In doing so, landlords not only enhance the property's value but also foster a sense of pride and connection among tenants and the surrounding community.

To ensure the successful execution of an ethically-minded property upgrade or renovation, thorough research and collaboration with professionals who share the same values is essential. This includes engaging architects, contractors, and suppliers who specialize in sustainable construction and design. Involving these experts from the initial planning stages to the final execution will help guarantee that the project aligns with your ethical principles as a landlord.

Additionally, maintaining open lines of communication with tenants throughout the upgrade or renovation process is paramount. Providing them with regular updates about the plans, expected timeline, and any temporary inconveniences will not only minimize complaints but also foster a sense of transparency and trust. Moreover, seeking input from tenants regarding their preferences or suggestions can establish a collaborative environment and enable you to tailor the upgrades to their specific needs.

When it comes to financing ethical property upgrades and renovations, it is important to explore available grants, tax incentives, or financing options that are specifically designed to support sustainable and ethical projects. Many governments and organizations offer financial assistance or subsidies for landlords who invest in eco-friendly and socially responsible renovations. By taking advantage of such opportunities, landlords can not only make a positive impact on the environment and tenants, but also benefit from long-term cost savings and increased property value.

Ethical property upgrades and renovations transcend mere functionality and aesthetics. They encompass considerations for environmental impact, tenant comfort, and the preservation of historical or cultural significance. As an ethical landlord, it is our responsibility to ensure that our properties are environmentally sustainable, provide a comfortable living experience for tenants, and contribute to the preservation of local heritage. By conducting thorough research, collaborating with professionals who share our values, and maintaining transparent communication with tenants, we can create properties that are not only ethically sound but also economically efficient and socially rewarding.

Tenant Education and Engagement

While implementing sustainable initiatives within rental properties is crucial, it is equally important to actively engage and educate tenants to ensure the success of these efforts. Tenant participation and buy-in are vital for maximizing the impact of sustainable practices and fostering a culture of environmental responsibility within the community.

One effective strategy for tenant education is the development of comprehensive sustainability guides or handbooks. These resources should provide tenants with clear and concise information about the property's sustainable features, such as energy-efficient appliances, water conservation measures, and recycling programs. Additionally, these guides can offer practical tips and advice on how tenants can contribute to these efforts through their daily habits and routines.

Regular workshops or informational sessions can also play a valuable role in tenant education. By hosting interactive events led by sustainability experts or knowledgeable staff members, tenants can gain a deeper understanding of the importance of sustainable living and learn about best practices tailored to their specific living environment. These workshops can cover topics such as energy conservation techniques, waste reduction strategies, and the benefits of sustainable transportation options.

Fostering a sense of community involvement and ownership is key to engaging tenants in sustainability initiatives. One way to achieve this is by establishing a "green team" or sustainability committee comprised of interested tenants. This group can serve as a liaison between the property management and the tenant community, providing feedback, organizing events, and championing sustainable initiatives. Empowering tenants to take an active role in decision-making and implementation can cultivate a sense of pride and accountability, ultimately leading to higher participation rates.

Incentive programs can also be effective in motivating tenants to adopt sustainable practices. For example, offering discounts or rewards for tenants who consistently demonstrate eco-friendly behaviors, such as recycling or conserving energy and water, can create a positive reinforcement system. Additionally, friendly competitions or challenges among tenants or buildings can foster a spirit of friendly rivalry and further encourage sustainable habits.

Transparency and regular communication are essential for maintaining tenant engagement. Providing regular updates on the property's sustainability performance, such as energy and water consumption data, recycling rates, or greenhouse gas emissions reductions, can help tenants understand the tangible impact of their actions. Celebrating milestones and successes can further reinforce the importance of these efforts and inspire continued participation.

It is also crucial to recognize and address potential barriers to tenant engagement. Language barriers, cultural differences, or economic constraints may hinder some tenants from fully participating in sustainability initiatives. By offering multi-lingual resources, tailoring programs to diverse needs, and providing affordable options, landlords can ensure that sustainability efforts are inclusive and accessible to all tenants.

Effective tenant education and engagement are critical components of a successful sustainable property management strategy. By providing comprehensive resources, hosting interactive workshops, fostering community involvement, offering incentives, maintaining transparency, and addressing potential barriers, landlords can empower tenants to become active participants in creating a more sustainable living environment. This collaborative approach not only maximizes the impact of eco-friendly initiatives but also cultivates a sense of pride, responsibility, and collective action towards a greener future.

Supporting Local Communities and Social Responsibility

First and foremost, the support of local communities involves the establishment of partnerships with local businesses. By engaging in collaboration with local businesses, not only does one contribute to the economic growth of the community but also cultivate a sense of unity and connection among residents. For instance, when seeking maintenance services for my properties, prioritizing the employment of local contractors and tradespeople is of paramount importance. This not only supports their livelihoods but also ensures that the revenue generated from rental properties circulates within the local economy, thereby benefiting everyone.

Furthermore, initiatives aimed at community engagement play a crucial role in the support of local communities. Such initiatives seek to establish a strong bond between tenants, neighbors, and myself as the landlord. One effective way in which this objective is achieved is by organizing community events and gatherings, such as barbecues or neighborhood clean-up days. These activities present an opportunity for tenants and residents to connect with one another, fostering a sense of belonging and camaraderie within the community. Additionally, they serve as a platform for open dialogue, enabling tenants to voice their concerns and suggestions about the property and the community as a whole.

To further support local communities, it is vital to acknowledge the power of charitable contributions. The act of giving back to society not only manifests as a moral obligation but also strengthens the social fabric of the community. One way in which I fulfill this duty is through collaborating with local charities and community organizations. For instance, organizing annual donation drives wherein tenants and community members are encouraged to contribute to causes such as food banks, shelters, or educational programs. These initiatives provide much-needed resources to those in need and foster a sense of altruism and empathy within the community.

It is important to note that supporting local communities through ethical property management practices not only benefits the community but also holds positive implications for the success and sustainability of my business. When tenants feel a sense of belonging and are part of a vibrant community, they are more inclined to reside in the property for an extended period. A sense of community encourages tenants to take pride in their living spaces, consequently resulting in a higher level of care and maintenance. Moreover, through the nurture of positive community relationships, a network of referrals and recommendations from content tenants becomes accessible, thus further enhancing the appeal of my properties.

One aspect of supporting local communities that necessitates careful deliberation is the potential for gentrification and its impact on vulnerable populations. Gentrification, wherein investment and renovation in underserved areas leads to increased property values and the displacement of low-income residents, can have adverse effects on the community. As a responsible and conscientious landlord, it is incumbent upon me to navigate this issue delicately and proactively.

To mitigate potential negative consequences, I collaborate closely with community organizations that are dedicated to affordable housing and advocate for policies that safeguard the rights of low-income residents. By engaging in dialogue with local authorities and remaining well-informed about the specific needs of the community, I can ensure that my business practices align with the principles of social responsibility.

Supporting local communities through ethical property management practices is not only a moral imperative but also a strategic business decision. By forging partnerships with local businesses, participating in community initiatives, and making charitable contributions, landlords can foster a sense of unity, connection, and pride within the community. Moreover, this support guarantees the long-term prosperity and viability of the property management business. As an ethical landlord, I am fully dedicated to implementing these practices and continuously exploring avenues to make a positive impact on the communities I serve.

Chapter 6: Effective Communication and Conflict Resolution

Clear and Transparent Communication

Throughout my experience as a landlord, I have recognized the significant importance of clear and transparent communication between landlords and tenants. Effective communication is fundamental in establishing trust, understanding, and cooperation in the landlord-tenant relationship.

Setting Expectations:

One of the initial and vital steps in maintaining clear and transparent communication is setting expectations from the outset. Before tenants move in, it is crucial to have a comprehensive discussion regarding the lease terms, rental payment arrangements, and any specific property rules or regulations. This establishes a common understanding and ensures both parties are on the same page.

Furthermore, it is important to encourage tenants to express their expectations and concerns. By actively listening to their needs and requirements, potential issues can be addressed early on, resulting in creative solutions that benefit both parties. Transparent discussions about any limitations or restrictions on property usage, such as pet policies or noise regulations, are crucial in preventing misunderstandings later.

Providing Timely Updates:

Communication should not cease once the lease agreement has been signed. As a responsible landlord, it is my aim to provide timely updates to tenants regarding any significant changes or developments that may affect their living situation. This includes informing them of repairs and maintenance work, changes in property management personnel, or updates to the lease agreement.

Of course, unexpected issues may arise during a tenant's stay, such as sudden appliance malfunctions or water leaks. In such cases, it is a priority to promptly inform the tenant, explaining the situation and outlining the steps being taken to resolve it. This level of transparency not only keeps the tenant informed but also demonstrates that their well-being is of utmost importance.

Addressing Concerns:

Effective communication requires an open and responsive approach. It is equally important to create an environment where tenants feel comfortable expressing their concerns or raising any issues they may have regarding the property. To facilitate this, tenants are encouraged to communicate via email, phone, or scheduled meetings. By establishing a safe and non-judgmental space for tenants to voice their concerns, prompt actions can be taken to address their needs and foster a positive and respectful living environment.

In some instances, tenants may hesitate to communicate their concerns due to fear of reprisal or a perceived power imbalance.

As a landlord, it is vital to actively cultivate trust with tenants, ensuring they feel heard and supported. Regular check-ins and proactive discussions to address potential grievances can help establish a strong foundation of trust and transparency.

In addition to addressing individual tenant concerns, facilitating open discussions within the tenant community is also beneficial. This can involve organizing monthly meetings or creating digital platforms, such as an online forum or a dedicated email group, for tenants to raise common issues or suggest improvements. Taking a proactive approach in collectively addressing these concerns allows for collaboration in creating a harmonious living space.

The Benefits of Clear and Transparent Communication:

Implementing clear and transparent communication practices between landlords and tenants yields numerous benefits. First and foremost, it establishes a foundation of trust and cooperation. When tenants feel that their concerns are being heard and addressed, they are more likely to comply with lease terms, take better care of the property, and stay for longer tenures.

Furthermore, by fostering an environment where tenants feel comfortable expressing their concerns, minor issues can be identified and resolved before they escalate into significant problems. This not only saves time and resources but also helps maintain the overall condition and value of the property.

Clear and transparent communication also plays a crucial role in financial aspects. When tenants are aware of any upcoming rent increases or changes in payment methods well in advance, it allows them to plan their finances accordingly, reducing stress and potential conflicts. Similarly, landlords benefit from timely communication on any maintenance or repair issues, enabling them to allocate resources and address problems promptly.

Ultimately, clear and transparent communication enhances the overall landlord-tenant relationship, ensuring a positive and beneficial living experience for both parties. By fostering an environment built on trust, understanding, and cooperation, landlords can cultivate a loyal and satisfied tenant base, reducing turnover rates and maximizing rental income.

Conclusion:

Clear and transparent communication is the foundation of a successful and ethical landlord. By setting expectations, providing timely updates, and addressing concerns, landlords can establish trust, foster cooperation, and create a harmonious living environment for tenants. This chapter highlights the importance of effective communication practices and provides valuable insights into how landlords can cultivate meaningful relationships with their tenants. Practicing clear and transparent communication is not only a professional responsibility but also a pathway to a thriving and sustainable landlord-tenant relationship.

Active Listening and Empathy

As a conscientious landlord, I have always believed that effective communication plays a pivotal role in maintaining a harmonious relationship with my tenants. Over the years, I have come to recognize that active listening and empathy are fundamental components in this equation. By truly comprehending the needs and concerns of my tenants, I am better equipped to attend to their issues and establish a just and ethical living environment for all parties involved.

Active listening surpasses simply hearing; it entails wholeheartedly dedicating one's attention to the speaker and comprehending their message. As an ethical landlord, it is my obligation to ensure that my tenants feel heard and appreciated. By actively listening, I can cultivate a sense of trust and open communication, which in turn cultivates a more favorable tenant-landlord relationship.

One of the most significant aspects of active listening is maintaining eye contact and providing verbal and non-verbal cues to indicate my full engagement in the conversation. When my tenants approach me with their concerns or problems, I make a conscious effort to provide them with my undivided attention. By doing so, I demonstrate that their concerns hold importance to me and that I am willing to listen and address their needs.

In addition to active listening, empathy is another indispensable element of effective communication. Empathy encompasses placing oneself in another person's shoes and comprehending their emotions and perspectives. As an ethical landlord, it is crucial for me to empathize with my tenants' experiences and challenges, as this enables me to implement fair and impartial solutions.

Being empathetic means acknowledging and validating my tenants' emotions, even if I may not personally share those same emotions. By attentively listening and responding with empathy, I create a secure space for my tenants to openly share their thoughts and concerns. This not only aids in conflict resolution but also allows me to gain a more profound understanding of their needs and make decisions that are equitable and principled.

Based on my experience, conflicts and misunderstandings are inevitable in any landlord-tenant relationship. However, through the utilization of active listening and empathy, I have discovered effective methods to address and resolve these issues in a just and ethical manner.

When faced with a conflict, I first ensure that I provide ample opportunity for both parties to express their concerns fully. This involves listening without interruption, posing clarifying questions, and reflecting back on what has been said to ensure accurate comprehension. By employing this process of active listening, I am able to gather information and obtain a better understanding of the underlying issues at hand.

Subsequently, I incorporate empathy by considering the perspectives and emotions of each party. By taking the time to comprehend the underlying reasons behind their actions or requests, I can empathize with their viewpoints and validate their sentiments. This not only aids in de-escalating tensions but also lays the groundwork for open and honest communication.

Once both parties have been heard and understood, I work towards finding a fair and ethical resolution. In some instances, this may involve compromise or negotiating terms that satisfy both parties. By consistently demonstrating fairness and transparency throughout the resolution process, I exemplify my commitment to establishing an ethical living environment that fosters harmony and respect.

It is imperative to note that active listening and empathy do not provide an assurance that all conflicts will be effortlessly resolved or to the satisfaction of everyone involved. However, by incorporating these practices into my communication approach, I am cultivating a culture of understanding, empathy, and equity.

Active listening and empathy serve as indispensable tools for effective communication, fostering understanding, and resolving conflicts in a fair and ethical manner as an ethical landlord. By actively listening to my tenants and demonstrating empathy towards their concerns, I establish a safe and respectful environment that encourages open communication and mutual comprehension. Through the adoption of these practices, I have found that conflicts can be more effectively addressed and resolved, thereby ensuring a harmonious tenant-landlord relationship.

Mediation and Alternative Dispute Resolution

Throughout my extensive experience as a landlord, I have encountered various conflicts between myself and my tenants, ranging from minor issues such as noise complaints to more significant matters such as rent disputes. It is crucial to acknowledge that conflicts are inevitable and cannot be completely avoided. However, the crucial aspect lies in the resolution of these conflicts and whether both parties can reach a mutually agreeable outcome. This is where mediation and alternative dispute resolution methods come into play.

Mediation is a process of facilitated negotiation that involves an impartial third party, known as a mediator, who assists the landlord and tenant in reaching a mutually satisfactory resolution to their conflict. It is a voluntary process that provides an opportunity for both parties to voice their concerns and actively engage in finding a solution. The mediator's role is not to impose decisions or express personal opinions, but rather to foster communication, clarify misunderstandings, and guide the parties towards a settlement.

One significant advantage of mediation is its promotion of open dialogue and encouragement of a cooperative mindset. It creates a non-adversarial environment where both the landlord and tenant can freely express their concerns and perspectives without fear of judgment or hostility. By allowing each party to voice their interests and grievances, mediation empowers them to actively participate in problem-solving. This collaborative approach fosters a sense of ownership and responsibility for the resolution, increasing the probability of a mutually satisfactory outcome.

Another benefit of mediation lies in its flexibility and adaptability to the specific needs of the landlord and tenant. Unlike traditional court proceedings, which adhere strictly to rules and procedures, mediation allows the parties to tailor their own solutions based on their unique circumstances. This flexibility enables creative problem-solving and encourages the exploration of alternatives that may not be available in a courtroom setting. By considering various options, the parties can discover innovative solutions that effectively address the underlying issues, ensuring a favorable outcome for both parties.

Moreover, mediation provides a cost-effective and time-efficient alternative to litigation. Court cases can be time-consuming, expensive, and emotionally draining for all involved parties. In contrast, mediation offers a quicker and more affordable way to resolve conflicts. The informal nature of mediation simplifies the process, reducing the time spent in legal proceedings. Additionally, since mediation is a voluntary process, the parties have control over the timing and scheduling, allowing them to reach a resolution at their own pace.

It is important to note the essential role of mediators, who are skilled professionals that maintain neutrality and impartiality. These individuals undergo specialized training to develop their mediation skills, including active listening, effective communication, and conflict resolution techniques. By remaining neutral and impartial, mediators create a safe and balanced environment for the parties to engage in constructive dialogue. Their role involves facilitating the conversation, guiding the parties towards common ground, and assisting them in exploring potential solutions. Mediators do not impose decisions upon the landlord and tenant; instead, they empower them to make their own choices.

Furthermore, alternative dispute resolution methods, such as arbitration, can also be highly advantageous in resolving conflicts between landlords and tenants. Arbitration is a process in which a neutral third party, known as an arbitrator, reviews the evidence and arguments presented by both parties and renders a binding decision. Unlike mediation, where the parties have control over the outcome, arbitration grants the arbitrator more control as they act as a judge based on the presented evidence.

Arbitration can be beneficial in situations where the parties are unable to reach an agreement through negotiation or mediation. It provides a structured process and a final resolution, ensuring closure for the parties and reducing the potential for further disputes. This method is particularly useful when addressing complex legal issues or when expeditious decision-making is required. Additionally, arbitration can be less costly and time-consuming compared to litigation, making it a viable alternative for efficiently resolving conflicts.

It is essential to emphasize that mediation and alternative dispute resolution methods should not replace the legal system but rather complement it. In certain cases, conflicts may be too intricate or substantial for mediation alone, necessitating the intervention of the court system. However, by encouraging the utilization of mediation and alternative dispute resolution methods as the initial step in conflict resolution, both landlords and tenants can save time, money, and emotional strain. Mediation can prevent minor disputes from escalating into full-blown legal battles, fostering better relationships and promoting positive landlord-tenant interactions.

Mediation and alternative dispute resolution methods offer numerous benefits in resolving conflicts between landlords and tenants. Through open dialogue, flexibility, cost-effectiveness, and active involvement of the parties, mediation empowers landlords and tenants to find mutually satisfactory solutions. Arbitration provides a binding decision when negotiation and mediation prove ineffective or impractical. By embracing these methods, landlords can cultivate a more harmonious rental community and establish a positive and ethical renting environment.

Dealing With Difficult Tenants Ethically

Being a landlord can present challenges, particularly when dealing with difficult tenants. As a responsible and ethical landlord, it is important to handle these situations with care and integrity. This chapter provides guidance on ethically dealing with difficult tenants, including strategies for addressing problematic behavior, establishing boundaries, and seeking professional assistance when necessary.

Understanding the underlying causes of difficult behavior is essential before taking any action. Personal problems, financial difficulties, mental health issues, or a lack of knowledge about appropriate conduct can all contribute to tenant misconduct. By empathizing with their circumstances, landlords can approach these situations with compassion.

Open and honest communication is the foundation of a healthy landlord-tenant relationship. When encountering problematic behavior, it is crucial to promptly address the issue. Private discussions with the tenant should express concerns about their behavior and its effects on other tenants and the property. This should be done in a caring and non-confrontational manner to encourage the tenant to reflect on their actions.

Establishing clear expectations and boundaries from the start is vital to avoid misunderstandings. These guidelines should be included in the lease agreement and thoroughly explained to the tenant. By establishing these boundaries, landlords create a framework for acceptable behavior, making it easier to address problematic situations in the future.

Recognizing that difficult behavior may stem from real-life challenges is equally important. Ethical landlords may consider offering support and informational resources to assist tenants in overcoming their difficulties. Connecting tenants with local organizations or services that provide financial management assistance, mental health counseling, or relevant support networks demonstrates ethical consideration.

Promptly and fairly addressing problematic behavior is crucial. Documenting each incident, including the time, date, and specific behavior displayed, is a recommended practice. Discussions with the tenant should involve pointing out specific issues, expressing concern, and discussing possible solutions.

If discussions fail to facilitate positive change, engaging a professional mediator may be beneficial. Mediation can foster a collaborative approach by clarifying concerns and exploring potential resolutions. A mediator serves as an impartial third party and ensures the interests of both the landlord and tenant are considered in finding a mutually satisfactory solution.

In situations where discussions and mediation are unsuccessful, enforcing consequences becomes necessary. However, it is crucial to approach this ethically and legally. Reviewing local tenancy laws and seeking legal advice, if necessary, ensures that imposed consequences are fair and within the landlord's legal rights.

In some cases, difficult tenants may require professional assistance beyond a landlord's expertise. In such instances, involving social services or mental health professionals may be necessary. While challenging, this step is essential for the overall welfare of all parties involved.

Eviction should always be seen as a last resort when all other ethical options have been explored. Before initiating eviction proceedings, seeking legal advice is recommended to verify its justifiability. It is important to approach eviction with empathy and respect, adhering to all legal obligations and providing tenants with sufficient notice.

Dealing with difficult tenants ethically calls for a compassionate and fair approach. Understanding the root causes of problematic behavior, practicing open and honest communication, establishing clear expectations, and offering support and resources enable landlords to create a conducive environment for positive change. When necessary, seeking mediation, enforcing consequences, or considering eviction must be conducted ethically and within legal parameters. The objective is to cultivate a harmonious living environment while upholding the rights and well-being of both tenants and landlords.

Building Positive Landlord-Tenant Relationships

Effective Communication, Trust-Building, and Fostering a Sense of Community within Rental Properties

As a landlord, I perceive the establishment of positive relationships with tenants as a crucial aspect of responsible and ethical property ownership. This not only cultivates a harmonious living environment but also ensures the long-term success of rental properties. This chapter aims to emphasize the significance of fostering positive relationships with tenants through effective communication, trust-building, and the development of a sense of community within rental properties.

Communication serves as the bedrock upon which all successful relationships are built, and the landlord-tenant relationship is no exception. Achieving effective communication necessitates both parties being open and transparent. However, as the landlord, I bear the responsibility of initiating and sustaining this line of communication. From the outset of the tenant screening process, I am meticulous in outlining my expectations and rental policies to avoid any misunderstandings. This entails the provision of clear and concise lease agreements that explicitly delineate the responsibilities of both the landlord and the tenant.

Moreover, in addition to establishing clear expectations, I believe in maintaining regular and open lines of communication with my tenants. This includes being responsive to their inquiries, concerns, and maintenance requests in a timely manner. To facilitate this, I ensure the availability of multiple communication channels, such as phone, email, and even social media, thereby enabling tenants to reach out to me through their preferred mode of communication. By demonstrating accessibility and responsiveness to their needs, I have observed that tenants are more inclined to place their trust in me and hold a favorable view of our landlord-tenant relationship.

Furthermore, trust-building constitutes another indispensable aspect of fostering a positive landlord-tenant relationship. As the landlord, I recognize that trust must be earned rather than assumed, and it is my obligation to establish a foundation of trust with my tenants. This commences by being honest and transparent in all interactions with tenants. From the rental application process to the handling of security deposits, I ensure complete transparency regarding all aspects of the rental property and the landlord-tenant relationship. Through comprehensive disclosure and steadfast reliability, I succeed in gaining the trust of my tenants, leading to a more positive and mutually beneficial relationship.

Equally essential to cultivating positive relationships with tenants is the creation of a sense of community within rental properties. I firmly believe that fostering a communal ambiance not only enriches the tenant's rental experience but also contributes to the overall prosperity and longevity of rental properties. To achieve this, I make concerted efforts to connect with my tenants beyond the confines of the landlord-tenant relationship. This entails organizing community events, such as barbecues or holiday parties, wherein tenants can interact with one another and cultivate a sense of belonging within the property.

Moreover, I actively encourage tenants' engagement in community activities, allowing them to establish relationships with their neighbors and foster a stronger support system within the property. Additionally, I actively promote clear and transparent lines of communication amongst tenants, whether by creating a bulletin board for announcement postings or facilitating the sharing of contact information among them. These measures foster greater connection and accountability among tenants, resulting in an augmented sense of pride and ownership.

Cultivating positive relationships with tenants transcends the mere collection of rent and encompasses the creation of a harmonious and mutually beneficial living environment. By prioritizing effective communication, trust-building, and the fostering of a sense of community within rental properties, landlords can greatly enhance the landlord-tenant relationship. This not only yields more contented tenants but also ensures the long-term prosperity and profitability of rental properties. As an ethical landlord, I am steadfastly committed to going above and beyond in establishing positive relationships with my tenants, as it lies at the core of responsible property ownership.

Cultural Competency in Landlord-Tenant Communication

In today's increasingly multicultural societies, it is essential for landlords to cultivate cultural competency when communicating with tenants from diverse backgrounds. Cultural competency refers to the ability to understand, appreciate, and effectively interact with people across cultures. By embracing this mindset, landlords can build stronger relationships, prevent misunderstandings, and create an inclusive living environment for all tenants.

One of the key aspects of cultural competency is recognizing and respecting cultural differences. Cultures can vary significantly in their values, beliefs, communication styles, and behavioral norms. What may be considered appropriate or respectful in one culture could be perceived as offensive or inappropriate in another. As a landlord, it is crucial to approach interactions with an open mind and a willingness to learn about and adapt to the cultural perspectives of your tenants.

Effective communication plays a pivotal role in bridging cultural divides. Language barriers can pose a significant challenge, particularly when dealing with tenants who are not fluent in the primary language used in the rental property. In such cases, landlords should explore options for providing written materials, such as lease agreements and notices, in the tenant's preferred language. Additionally, engaging professional interpretation services during important meetings or discussions can ensure clear and accurate communication.

It is equally important to be mindful of non-verbal communication cues, as these can vary across cultures. Maintaining eye contact, personal space, gestures, and body language can have different meanings and implications in different cultural contexts. By being attentive to these subtle nuances, landlords can avoid unintentional misunderstandings and foster a more respectful and inclusive environment.

Moreover, cultural competency extends beyond language and communication styles; it also encompasses understanding and respecting cultural traditions, beliefs, and practices. For example, certain religious or cultural groups may have specific dietary restrictions, dress codes, or observances that should be acknowledged and accommodated within reason. By demonstrating a willingness to learn and accommodate these cultural practices, landlords can build trust and rapport with their tenants.

Ongoing education and training are essential for developing and maintaining cultural competency. Landlords can seek out resources such as cultural awareness workshops, online courses, or partnerships with local cultural organizations. These opportunities can provide valuable insights into different cultures, helping landlords to better understand and appreciate the diversity within their tenant communities.

Additionally, fostering open and respectful dialogue with tenants can be a powerful tool for enhancing cultural competency. Encouraging tenants to share their cultural backgrounds, traditions, and perspectives can not only facilitate mutual understanding but also create opportunities for landlords to learn and grow in their cultural awareness.

Embracing cultural competency in landlord-tenant communication is not only an ethical responsibility but also a strategic investment in building positive and inclusive living environments. By respecting cultural differences, addressing language barriers, understanding non-verbal cues, accommodating cultural practices, and continuously seeking to learn and grow, landlords can create an atmosphere of trust, respect, and mutual understanding with their diverse tenant communities. This approach not only enhances the quality of life for tenants but also contributes to the long-term success and sustainability of rental properties.

Leveraging Technology for Effective

Communication and Record-Keeping

In today's digital age, the integration of technology into landlord-tenant communication has become increasingly prevalent and valuable. From online portals and mobile apps to social media platforms, these tools offer numerous advantages in streamlining communication, maintaining detailed records, and mitigating potential disputes.

Online Tenant Portals Implementing a secure online tenant portal can revolutionize the way landlords communicate and share information with their tenants. These portals serve as a centralized hub where tenants can access important documents, such as lease agreements, policies, and community announcements. Additionally, portals often feature messaging systems that enable efficient two-way communication between landlords and tenants, facilitating the prompt resolution of inquiries or maintenance requests.

Mobile Apps Mobile applications designed specifically for property management can further enhance communication and accessibility. These apps typically offer features like maintenance request submission, rent payment options, and real-time updates on community events or building notices. By putting these capabilities at tenants' fingertips, landlords can foster a more responsive and transparent communication experience.

Social Media Platforms While social media platforms should not be the primary means of official communication, they can serve as valuable supplementary channels. Establishing a presence on platforms like Facebook, Twitter, or Instagram can allow landlords to share community updates, event information, and general announcements with tenants in a more informal and engaging manner.

Detailed Record-Keeping One of the significant advantages of leveraging technology for landlord-tenant communication is the ability to maintain accurate and detailed records. Online portals, mobile apps, and even email correspondence create digital trails that can be invaluable in the event of disputes or misunderstandings.

For instance, if a tenant claims they did not receive a specific notice or communication, landlords can easily retrieve timestamped records of when the message was sent and potentially even when it was viewed or opened by the recipient. This level of documentation can help prevent "he said, she said" situations and provide clear evidence to support the landlord's actions.

Dispute Resolution In the unfortunate event of a dispute between a landlord and tenant, having a comprehensive record of all communication can be crucial in resolving the matter fairly and efficiently. Digital records can serve as valuable evidence in mediation or legal proceedings, allowing both parties to present a clear timeline of events and interactions.

Additionally, some online platforms and applications offer built-in dispute resolution features, such as the ability to upload and share documents, schedule mediation sessions, or even facilitate online arbitration processes. These technological tools can streamline the dispute resolution process, reducing the need for lengthy administrative procedures or costly legal battles.

Privacy and Security Considerations While embracing technology for communication offers numerous advantages, it is essential for landlords to prioritize the privacy and security of tenant information. Online portals, mobile apps, and communication channels should be equipped with robust security measures, such as encryption, multi-factor authentication, and strict access controls, to safeguard sensitive data from unauthorized access or breaches.

Furthermore, landlords should be transparent about their data collection and usage practices, ensuring compliance with relevant privacy laws and regulations. Obtaining explicit consent from tenants for the collection and storage of personal information is crucial, and tenants should be informed about their rights regarding data access, rectification, and erasure.

By leveraging technology for communication, such as online portals, mobile apps, and social media platforms, landlords can streamline interactions with tenants, maintain comprehensive records, and more effectively mitigate potential disputes. However, it is imperative to balance these benefits with a steadfast commitment to privacy, security, and ethical data handling practices. When implemented thoughtfully and responsibly, technology can become a powerful ally in fostering effective, transparent, and well-documented communication between landlords and tenants.

Setting Boundaries and Establishing Professional Boundaries

While open and respectful communication is essential in the landlord-tenant relationship, it is equally important to establish clear boundaries and maintain a professional demeanor. These boundaries not only protect the interests of both parties but also prevent misunderstandings and potential conflicts.

Defining Professional Boundaries Professional boundaries refer to the appropriate limits and guidelines that govern the interactions between landlords and tenants. These boundaries ensure that the relationship remains respectful, ethical, and focused on the specific terms and conditions outlined in the lease agreement.

Some key aspects of professional boundaries in the landlord-tenant relationship include:

1. Maintaining a clear separation between personal and professional matters: It is crucial to avoid discussing or involving personal matters that are unrelated to the rental agreement or property management. This helps prevent potential conflicts of interest or inappropriate situations.

2. Respecting privacy and personal space: Landlords should respect the privacy of tenants and their living spaces. Entering a tenant's unit without proper notice or valid reason is a violation of their personal space and can damage the trust in the relationship.

3. Avoiding favoritism or discrimination: Treating all tenants fairly and without bias or favoritism is essential. Landlords must ensure that their actions and decisions are based on objective criteria and not influenced by personal preferences or prejudices.
4. Refraining from inappropriate or unethical behavior: Any form of harassment, intimidation, or unethical conduct towards tenants is strictly unacceptable. Landlords must maintain a professional and respectful demeanor at all times.

Establishing Boundaries from the Start It is recommended to clearly outline the boundaries and expectations of the landlord-tenant relationship from the very beginning. This can be achieved by including a section on professional conduct and boundaries in the lease agreement or tenant handbook.

By explicitly stating the expectations for appropriate behavior, communication channels, and the limits of the relationship, landlords can set the tone for a professional and respectful dynamic with their tenants.

Maintaining Open and Respectful Communication While boundaries are necessary, it is equally important to foster open and respectful communication with tenants. Effective communication not only helps resolve issues promptly but also contributes to a positive and harmonious living environment.

Landlords should encourage tenants to voice their concerns or inquiries through designated channels, such as email, phone, or scheduled meetings. It is essential to respond to these communications in a timely and professional manner, addressing the issues at hand without overstepping personal boundaries.

Regular check-ins or tenant meetings can also be beneficial in maintaining open lines of communication. These forums provide an opportunity for landlords and tenants to discuss any concerns, address maintenance issues, or clarify policies and procedures in a respectful and transparent manner.

Addressing Boundary Violations Despite best efforts, boundary violations may occur in some instances. It is crucial for landlords to address these situations promptly and professionally.

If a tenant violates boundaries by engaging in inappropriate behavior or overstepping personal limits, the landlord should address the issue directly but respectfully. This can involve a private conversation or a formal written warning, depending on the severity of the violation.

In cases where the boundary violation is severe or recurring, landlords may need to consider more stringent measures, such as terminating the lease agreement or seeking legal assistance. However, it is essential to follow proper legal procedures and documentation to avoid any potential liabilities.

The "Other Ways" to Pay Rent Misconception It is important to address the misconception portrayed in some media regarding inappropriate arrangements between landlords and tenants. The notion of tenants offering or suggesting "other ways" to pay rent, often depicted in adult entertainment, is not only unethical but also illegal in most jurisdictions.

Engaging in such arrangements can lead to numerous legal and ethical complications, including:

1. Potential for exploitation or coercion: Power dynamics in the landlord-tenant relationship can create situations where tenants may feel pressured or coerced into agreeing to inappropriate arrangements, even if they are initially presented as consensual.
2. Legal ramifications: Depending on the jurisdiction, engaging in such arrangements could constitute illegal activities, such as solicitation or prostitution, which carry severe legal consequences for both parties.
3. Damage to professional reputation: If such arrangements were to become public knowledge, it could severely damage the reputation and credibility of the landlord, making it difficult to attract and retain ethical tenants in the future.
4. Emotional and psychological impact: Engaging in inappropriate arrangements can have significant emotional and psychological consequences for both parties, potentially leading to feelings of guilt, shame, or trauma.
5. Breach of trust and ethical standards: Such arrangements violate the trust and ethical standards expected in the landlord-tenant relationship, undermining the foundation of a professional and

respectful dynamic.

It is crucial for landlords to maintain the highest ethical standards and avoid any temptation or suggestion of engaging in inappropriate arrangements related to rent payments or other aspects of the relationship. Professionalism, respect, and adherence to legal and ethical boundaries should be the guiding principles in all interactions with tenants.

By establishing clear boundaries, maintaining open and respectful communication, and addressing potential boundary violations promptly and professionally, landlords can cultivate a healthy and positive landlord-tenant relationship built on trust, integrity, and mutual respect.

Chapter 7: Ethical Financial Management for Landlords

Transparent Financial Reporting

As a landlord, my primary objective is to provide my tenants with a secure and comfortable living environment. However, I also believe that ethical landlord practices extend beyond meeting the minimum standards. It encompasses the implementation of transparent financial reporting measures that enable trust and reliability between myself and my tenants. This chapter aims to explore the significance of transparent financial reporting, with a particular focus on issuing clear rent statements, responsibly managing security deposits, and maintaining accurate records.

First and foremost, transparent financial reporting is crucial for fostering a healthy landlord-tenant relationship. A fundamental aspect of this transparency involves providing tenants with clear and concise rent statements. These statements should contain comprehensive information about the rent amount, due date, as well as any additional charges or fees. By presenting this information transparently, tenants can easily comprehend the breakdown of their payments. This not only minimizes the possibility of misunderstandings and disputes, but also allows tenants to budget effectively and plan their expenses accordingly.

In order to guarantee the accuracy and transparency of rent statements, I put in place a meticulous system that records all financial transactions associated with my rental properties. This includes appropriately labeling each rent payment with the tenant's name, unit number, and date of payment. This system enables me to cross-reference these records with the rent statements provided to tenants, ensuring that any inconsistencies or inaccuracies can be promptly identified, addressed, and rectified.

Another crucial aspect of transparent financial reporting is the responsible handling of security deposits. Security deposits represent a significant financial commitment for tenants, and it is vital that they have confidence in their preservation. To ensure transparency, I provide tenants with a comprehensive breakdown of any deductions made from their security deposit at the end of their lease term. This breakdown includes an itemized list of repair costs or outstanding balances, supported by receipts or invoices. By being transparent about the deductions, tenants are able to comprehend the reasons for the specific amounts deducted and can address any concerns or disputes that may arise.

In addition to issuing clear rent statements and responsibly managing security deposits, maintaining accurate records is equally essential for transparent financial reporting. Precise record-keeping empowers me to effectively manage my finances, monitor the income and expenses associated with each rental unit, and ensure compliance with tax regulations. By meticulously documenting financial transactions, including rent payments and related expenses, I can readily provide tenants with any requested financial information, such as rent payment history, while also demonstrating the responsible utilization of their rent payments.

Moreover, transparent financial reporting also enhances the credibility and professionalism of my property management business. By providing clear and accurate financial information, tenants are more likely to deem me a trustworthy and reliable landlord. In turn, this can result in positive word-of-mouth referrals and increased tenant satisfaction, ultimately benefiting my business in the long term.

To uphold transparency in financial reporting, I prioritize the accessibility of all relevant financial information to my tenants. I make it a priority to offer tenants access to an online portal where they can view and download their rent statements and payment history. This platform allows for round-the-clock access to information, ensuring greater convenience and transparency. Additionally, I am always available to address any questions or concerns relating to financial matters that tenants may have, further reinforcing the transparency of my financial reporting practices.

In conclusion, transparent financial reporting plays a critical role in cultivating trust and reliability between landlords and tenants. By issuing clear rent statements, responsibly managing security deposits, and maintaining accurate records, I am able to ensure that my tenants possess a lucid comprehension of their financial obligations and can trust in the management of their financial transactions. This transparency not only benefits the tenants but also increases the credibility and professionalism of my property management business. By prioritizing transparent financial reporting, I cultivate stronger relationships with my tenants, leading to a more harmonious and mutually beneficial landlord-tenant experience.

Ethical Tax Planning and Compliance

Firstly, let us explore the concept of ethical tax planning for landlords. Tax planning involves strategically managing finances to minimize tax liabilities within the legal parameters. While landlords are entitled to engage in tax planning to lessen their tax burdens, it is crucial to differentiate between ethical and unethical practices.

One ethical consideration in tax planning as a landlord is transparency. It is incumbent upon me to be forthright and open with tax authorities regarding the income derived from my rental properties. This necessitates accurately reporting rental income on my tax returns and furnishing all requisite documentation to substantiate my claims. By maintaining transparency, I not only comply with tax regulations but also demonstrate integrity in my financial transactions.

Another ethical facet of tax planning involves abstaining from any aggressive or abusive tax strategies. This encompasses exploiting loopholes, partaking in fraudulent schemes, or intentionally misleading tax authorities to evade taxes. As an ethical landlord, I choose to strictly adhere to the law and refrain from engaging in any unethical practices. It is my belief that by honoring my tax obligations, I contribute to the societal welfare and support the essential public services funded by taxation.

Compliance with tax regulations is another crucial element of upholding ethical practices in tax planning as a landlord. By staying informed about tax laws, regulations, and updates, I can ensure that I fulfill my obligations and avoid unintentional non-compliance. This entails being aware of tax return filing deadlines, comprehending the allowable deductions and credits accessible to owners of rental properties, and maintaining clear and organized records of my financial transactions.

A key aspect of ethical tax planning is understanding the deductions and credits accessible to owners of rental properties. By availing of these legitimate tax benefits, I can reduce my tax liabilities while operating within the confines of the law. Some common deductions for rental property owners include property management fees, expenditures on repairs and maintenance, insurance premiums, and mortgage interest payments. Maintaining precise documentation and receipts for these expenses is crucial to substantiating their deductibility.

Moreover, there are tax credits available to rental property owners that can further decrease their tax obligations. For instance, the Low-Income Housing Tax Credit is a credit provided to landlords who offer affordable housing to low-income individuals or families. This program acts as an incentive for landlords to provide affordable rental units and assists them in offsetting their tax liabilities. By understanding and utilizing these credits, I can ensure that I maximize my tax planning efforts in an ethical manner.

Engaging in ethical tax planning practices, adhering to tax regulations, and understanding the deductions and credits available to landlords are vital components of being an ethical landlord. By practicing transparency, refraining from unethical tax strategies, and remaining compliant with tax laws, I can navigate the intricacies of tax planning in an ethical manner. Furthermore, by taking advantage of legitimate deductions and credits, I can minimize my tax liabilities while operating as a responsible landlord. As I continue to uphold ethical tax planning and compliance, I am confident that I positively contribute to both my own financial well-being and society at large.

Fair and Reasonable Fee Structures

As an accountable and ethical landlord, it is imperative to thoroughly consider the fee structures that are imposed on our tenants. Common practices in the rental industry such as application fees, late payment fees, and service charges must be approached in a fair, reasonable, and transparent manner.

Issue:

Application Fees

The initial fee tenants encounter when applying for a rental property is the application fee. While it is understandable that landlords incur expenses for processing applications and conducting background checks, a balance must be struck between covering these costs and burdening potential tenants with excessive fees.

Resolution:

Regard for fair and reasonable application fees is paramount. By conducting thorough research regarding local rental markets and industry standards, an appropriate application fee can be determined that covers necessary expenses without becoming an undue financial obstacle for prospective tenants. Transparency plays a vital role as well - clearly outlining the purpose and amount of the application fee fosters trust and ensures fairness.

Late Payment Fees

Late payment fees are often implemented as an incentive for tenants to submit their rent on time. However, it is crucial to approach this fee structure ethically, taking into account tenants' circumstances and financial capabilities.

Resolution:

Applying late payment fees must be done with empathy and understanding. By establishing open lines of communication with tenants, a relationship built on trust can be cultivated, allowing for collaborative problem-solving if financial difficulties arise. Implementing a grace period, wherein tenants are given a specific timeframe to make their payment without incurring additional fees, can also be a fair approach. Furthermore, an evaluation of the late payment fee amount is necessary to ensure it is reasonable and does not unduly burden tenants who are already facing financial challenges.

Service Charges

Service charges encompass various fees for maintenance, repairs, and utilities. These charges significantly impact the monthly expenses of tenants and require ethical consideration.

Resolution:

To approach service charges ethically, transparency is crucial. A clear breakdown of the charges and the services they cover ensures that tenants understand the basis for their payments. Regularly reviewing service charges to ensure they align with the actual cost of providing the services contributes to preventing tenants from being burdened with excessive charges, thereby maintaining transparency in fee structures.

Ethical approaches to fee structures, including application fees, late payment fees, and service charges, require prioritizing fairness, reasonableness, and transparency. By comprehending the needs and financial capabilities of our tenants, undertaking research on industry standards, and facilitating open lines of communication, our fee structures can align with ethical principles.

As responsible landlords, we bear the responsibility of creating a rental experience that is fair and respectful. Transparent fee structures that do not impose undue financial burdens on our tenants are a fundamental component of this endeavor. By implementing these ethical approaches to fee structures, we can foster a positive landlord-tenant relationship, uphold our reputation, and contribute to a more sustainable and ethical rental industry.

As I continue to evolve in my role as a landlord, I am committed to regularly reviewing and evaluating my fee structures, always striving for fairness, reasonableness, and transparency. It is through these ethical practices that I firmly believe we can create a more equitable and compassionate rental experience for all parties involved.

Avoiding Financial Exploitation of Tenants

Introduction:

As conscientious landlords, it is imperative that we fulfill our obligation of providing secure and affordable housing for all tenants. However, in addition to addressing the physical aspects of housing, we must also ensure that tenants are safeguarded against any form of financial mistreatment. This chapter will explore the various strategies landlords can employ to uphold their ethical duties by refraining from participating in predatory lending practices, avoiding unfair fees, and promoting transparent financial agreements.

1. Predatory Lending Practices:

1.1 Understanding Predatory Lending Practices:

Predatory lending practices encompass unethical and exploitative methods employed by certain lenders to take advantage of vulnerable tenants. Such practices often involve exorbitant interest rates, deceptive information dissemination, and aggressive tactics that coerce tenants into entering unfavorable loan agreements. As ethical landlords, it is crucial to be well-informed about these practices and take the necessary measures to protect our tenants.

1.2 Identifying Predatory Lenders:

To safeguard tenants against predatory lending practices, it is vital to identify lenders who engage in such behavior. Conducting thorough research and selecting reputable lending institutions that adhere to ethical lending standards is the initial step. Additionally, staying current on industry news, monitoring loan terms offered to tenants, and approaching lenders who push immediate decision-making with skepticism can help mitigate the risks associated with predatory lending.

2. Unfair Fees:

2.1 Recognizing Unfair Fees:

Many tenants often bear the burden of unfair fees, which not only exacerbate their financial strain but also establish an atmosphere of exploitation. As ethical landlords, it is our responsibility to ensure that tenants are not subjected to these unjust practices. Examples of unfair fees include excessive late fees, non-refundable fees lacking reasonable justification, and charges for services traditionally considered the landlord's responsibility.

2.2 Eliminating Unfair Fees:

To prevent the financial exploitation of tenants through unfair fees, it is essential to establish clear guidelines and policies concerning fees. All fees should be disclosed and explained before tenants sign a lease agreement to ensure full comprehension. Furthermore, consider eliminating non-essential fees and adopting a tenant-friendly approach by providing flexible payment options or reasonable grace periods for rent payments.

3. Transparent Financial Agreements:

3.1 Importance of Transparency:

Transparent financial agreements are paramount in maintaining an ethical landlord-tenant relationship. These agreements ensure that tenants are fully aware of their financial obligations, rights, and responsibilities. By promoting transparency, landlords can foster a culture of trust and fairness, thereby diminishing the risk of tenant exploitation.

3.2 Clarity in Lease Agreements:

An imperative step towards achieving transparent financial agreements is crafting clear and concise lease agreements. Avoid using complex language or legal jargon that can confuse tenants. Instead, utilize simple and easily understandable terms to outline payment schedules, rent increases, and other financial obligations. Encouraging tenants to seek clarification and providing the option for legal counsel, if necessary, can further enhance transparency.

3.3 Open Communication:

Open communication is vital for maintaining transparent financial agreements. Encourage tenants to voice any concerns they may have regarding financial matters. Be readily available to discuss payment plans, rent increases, or any other financial aspects of their tenancy. Consistently updating tenants on any changes in financial policies or agreements will help promote an environment of transparency and trust.

Conclusion:

Preventing the financial exploitation of tenants is an ethical imperative for landlords. By emphasizing the ethical responsibility to refrain from predatory lending practices, avoid unfair fees, and uphold transparent financial agreements, we can ensure that tenants are treated with dignity and respect. Upholding these principles not only reinforces the ethical standards of our profession but also cultivates a positive and mutually beneficial relationship between landlords and tenants.

Philanthropic Financial Practices

As a landlord who places great value on giving back to the community and making a positive impact, I have always regarded philanthropic financial practices as an integral part of my role. In this chapter, we will examine the numerous benefits that arise from implementing philanthropic initiatives as a landlord, including charitable contributions, affordable housing initiatives, and support for tenant financial literacy programs.

Charitable contributions, involving the donation of funds or resources to charitable organizations, can have a profound effect on both the recipients and the landlord. These contributions not only support important causes but also contribute to overall well-being and community development. Through consistent donations of a portion of rental income to reputable charities, I have been able to make a difference in the lives of less fortunate individuals, while also fostering goodwill among my tenants and the broader community.

One significant advantage of charitable contributions as a landlord is the positive perception it generates among tenants. When tenants are aware that a portion of their rent is going towards charitable causes, they feel a sense of pride and satisfaction in belonging to a caring community. This sense of community fosters a positive, supportive environment, resulting in happier and more engaged tenants. Content tenants are more likely to stay longer and treat the property with respect, ultimately reducing vacancies and maintenance costs.

Another benefit of philanthropic financial practices is the potential for tax advantages. In many countries, including the United States, landlords can deduct charitable donations from their annual income taxes. This not only lowers their tax liability but also presents an opportunity to redirect the savings towards property improvements or other investments. It is crucial to seek guidance from a tax professional to ensure compliance with local tax laws and maximize the benefits of charitable deductions.

Affordable housing initiatives, such as offering discounted rent or implementing income-based rent structures, are another philanthropic practice that can be highly advantageous for both landlords and tenants. By providing affordable housing options, landlords contribute to the overall well-being of the community by addressing housing inequality and reducing homelessness.

From a landlord's perspective, implementing affordable housing initiatives comes with multiple advantages. Firstly, it establishes a positive reputation and enhances the property's appeal to potential tenants. Individuals burdened by high living costs actively seek out affordable housing options, and by offering such options, landlords can ensure a steady stream of tenants and minimize vacancies.

Furthermore, affordable housing initiatives often come with government subsidies or tax breaks. Governments worldwide acknowledge the importance of affordable housing and offer incentives to landlords who participate in these programs. By taking advantage of these incentives, landlords can offset the costs associated with offering affordable housing and improve their overall financial situation.

Supporting tenant financial literacy programs is yet another philanthropic financial practice that can yield far-reaching benefits. Financial literacy is a critical skill that many individuals lack, and by providing resources and education to tenants, landlords empower them to make well-informed financial decisions.

One significant advantage of supporting tenant financial literacy programs is the reduction in instances of payment defaults and evictions. When tenants possess knowledge about money management, budgeting, and credit, they are more likely to prioritize rental payments and uphold their tenancy. This, in turn, reduces the financial burden on the landlord and enhances overall rental income stability.

Moreover, financially literate tenants are more likely to augment their income over time, leading to improved rental affordability and a greater ability to meet rent obligations. By supporting their financial growth, landlords can foster long-term tenant relationships and establish a sense of loyalty and trust.

Philanthropic financial practices can greatly benefit landlords, tenants, and the community as a whole. Through charitable contributions, affordable housing initiatives, and support for tenant financial literacy programs, landlords can not only make a positive impact but also reap various rewards, such as content tenants, tax advantages, reduced vacancies, improved financial stability, and an enhanced reputation. As landlords, it is not solely our responsibility to provide shelter, but also to contribute to the greater good and create a positive impact in the lives of our tenants and communities.

Proactive Financial Planning, Budgeting, and Risk Management Strategies

Effective financial management as an ethical landlord extends beyond transparent reporting and compliance - it necessitates a proactive approach to financial planning, budgeting, and risk mitigation. By implementing comprehensive strategies in these areas, landlords can safeguard their investments, maintain financial stability, and uphold their commitment to responsible property management.

Financial Planning and Budgeting Developing a robust financial plan is crucial for landlords to achieve long-term success while adhering to ethical practices. This process begins with accurately forecasting income and expenses associated with each rental property. Income projections should account for potential vacancy periods, rent increases or decreases based on market trends, and any anticipated changes in the tenant composition. On the expense side, landlords must diligently estimate costs such as property taxes, insurance premiums, utilities, routine maintenance, and capital improvements.

Once income and expense forecasts are established, landlords can create detailed budgets that allocate funds appropriately. Effective budgeting ensures that sufficient resources are allocated for essential expenses, such as repairs and maintenance, while also setting aside reserves for unexpected costs or emergencies. Maintaining adequate reserves is particularly important for ethical landlords, as it allows them to address unforeseen issues promptly without compromising tenant safety or quality of life.

Regular review and adjustment of financial plans and budgets are also necessary to account for changes in market conditions, regulatory environments, or tenant turnover. Landlords should remain vigilant and adapt their strategies as needed, always prioritizing transparency and open communication with tenants regarding any potential impacts on rental rates or service levels.

Risk Management and Insurance As with any investment, rental properties are subject to various risks that can threaten their financial viability and the well-being of tenants. Ethical landlords must proactively identify and mitigate these risks through comprehensive risk management strategies and appropriate insurance coverage.

One of the primary risks landlords face is property damage caused by natural disasters, fires, or accidents. To mitigate this risk, landlords should obtain adequate property insurance coverage that accounts for the replacement value of the building, as well as any necessary repairs or temporary housing arrangements for displaced tenants. Regular property inspections and preventive maintenance can also help identify and address potential hazards before they escalate into costly damages.

Liability risks represent another significant concern for landlords. Tenants or visitors who suffer injuries on the premises due to negligence or hazardous conditions may seek legal recourse, potentially resulting in costly lawsuits and settlements. Ethical landlords should carry sufficient liability insurance to protect themselves and their tenants in such situations. Additionally, implementing robust safety protocols, maintaining detailed records of inspections and repairs, and promptly addressing any reported hazards can help mitigate liability risks.

Business interruption risks, such as extended vacancy periods or temporary loss of rental income due to unforeseen circumstances, can also threaten a landlord's financial stability.

Landlords may consider obtaining business interruption insurance to safeguard against such risks and ensure continuity of operations.

Furthermore, ethical landlords should consider implementing risk management strategies that extend beyond insurance coverage. This may include conducting comprehensive background checks on potential tenants, implementing strict lease agreements and enforcing policies consistently, and fostering open communication with tenants to address concerns or issues promptly.

By integrating proactive financial planning, budgeting, and risk management strategies, ethical landlords can navigate the complexities of rental property ownership while upholding their commitment to responsible stewardship. Accurate forecasting, diligent budgeting, and adequate insurance coverage not only protect the landlord's investment but also ensure the safety, well-being, and financial stability of their tenants. Ultimately, this holistic approach to financial management reinforces the ethical principles of transparency, fairness, and accountability that define responsible landlordship.

Chapter 8: Continuous Learning and Improvement as an Ethical Landlord

Staying Updated on Landlord-Tenant Laws and Regulations

Neglecting to stay updated can have severe consequences. The excuse of being unaware of the law holds no weight and can result in expensive lawsuits, fines, and damage to your reputation as a landlord. These legal matters can place strain on your business and even lead to its destruction, not to mention the harm caused to your tenants.

To mitigate these risks, it is imperative for landlords to actively seek knowledge through legal resources and professional networks. In terms of legal resources, there exists a vast selection of materials that offer valuable insights into landlord-tenant laws and regulations. From my personal experience, books, websites, and articles solely dedicated to this subject provide invaluable sources of information.

One highly recommended book is "The Complete Guide to Landlord-Tenant Law" by Emily Doskow. This comprehensive guide covers various topics, including tenant screening, lease agreements, eviction procedures, and more. Doskow's book is written in easily comprehensible language and offers practical tips and real-life examples, aiding landlords in navigating the complexities of the legal environment.

In addition to books, websites such as government-run housing authorities and legal databases also offer a wealth of information. These websites grant access to local, state, and federal laws, court cases, and regulations that are applicable to landlord-tenant relationships. Familiarizing yourself with these resources and regularly checking for updates will ensure you remain informed and compliant.

Another effective strategy is to join professional networks and organizations that center around landlord-tenant issues. These groups provide a platform for networking with fellow landlords, property managers, and legal professionals. Through active participation in discussions, attendance at seminars, and the sharing of experiences, valuable insights into best practices are gained while remaining up to date with industry changes.

One exceptional network that has proven immensely helpful is the National Association of Residential Property Managers (NARPM). This organization offers resources, educational programs, and networking opportunities tailored specifically to address the needs of landlords and property managers. Joining such a network not only keeps you informed but also enhances professional growth, credibility, and reputation.

In addition to legal resources and networks, it is crucial to consult with legal professionals specializing in landlord-tenant law. While books and websites provide a wealth of knowledge, there may be specific situations or nuances in your local jurisdiction that necessitate expert advice. Establishing a relationship with a trusted attorney experienced in this field can offer peace of mind, knowing professional guidance is readily available.

When seeking legal advice, it is essential to select an attorney with thorough understanding of landlord-tenant laws in your specific area. State and local laws can vary significantly, and a generalist attorney may lack the specialized knowledge required to navigate these intricacies. It is important to invest time and effort in researching and interviewing attorneys focusing on real estate and landlord-tenant law in order to ensure you have the best counsel at your disposal.

Lastly, the significance of not only acquiring knowledge but also acting upon it cannot be overstated. Being informed about landlord-tenant laws and regulations is one thing, but implementing them within your rental business is equally crucial. Constructing transparent and legally compliant lease agreements, adhering to fair housing laws, conducting regular property inspections, and promptly addressing maintenance issues are all vital aspects of responsible property management.

Remaining updated on landlord-tenant laws and regulations is a fundamental element of being an ethical and responsible landlord. By proactively seeking knowledge through legal resources and professional networks, landlords can safeguard their business and ensure the well-being of their tenants. Investing time and effort into staying informed will ultimately yield benefits such as smoother relations with tenants, reduced legal risks, and a positive industry reputation. A complete ethical landlord encompasses being well-versed in the law and ensuring compliance in all aspects of the rental business.

Seeking Feedback From Tenants

Seeking feedback from tenants holds utmost importance in the realm of property management. While maintaining a clean and well-kept property is crucial for tenant satisfaction, establishing an open and transparent line of communication between the landlord and tenant is equally significant. This is where the act of seeking feedback becomes paramount.

The primary purpose of seeking feedback is to identify areas that require improvement. No matter how well-maintained a property may be, there is always room for enhancement. By actively soliciting feedback from tenants, valuable insights can be gained regarding aspects of the property that could benefit from improvement. It could range from necessary repairs to the improvement of common areas, or even suggestions for additional amenities that would enhance the overall living experience. Failing to seek feedback means missing out on these opportunities for improvement.

Seeking feedback also allows for prompt addressing of any concerns or issues raised by tenants. It is crucial for tenants to feel heard and valued, and by actively seeking their feedback, landlords can demonstrate their commitment to addressing any concerns that may arise. Whether it involves resolving maintenance issues, resolving problems with neighbors, or addressing any other issue related to tenancy, seeking feedback enables landlords to take prompt and effective action to ensure the peace of mind and satisfaction of their tenants.

Apart from addressing concerns and improving the property, seeking feedback also helps in enhancing the overall rental experience. Regularly connecting with tenants and gathering their feedback provides landlords with a deeper understanding of their wants, needs, and preferences. This knowledge enables landlords to tailor their services and offerings to better meet tenant expectations. It could involve implementing new amenities, organizing community events, or simply adopting a more personalized approach to property management. Seeking feedback is instrumental in creating an environment that truly makes the living experience enjoyable for tenants.

Nevertheless, the question arises as to how landlords can effectively seek feedback from tenants? Simply asking generic questions like "How are things?" or "Is everything okay?" does not elicit the depth of feedback required for meaningful improvement. Instead, a step-by-step guide has been devised to effectively seek feedback:

Step 1: Foster an open and approachable relationship with tenants from the outset. By creating an environment where tenants feel comfortable sharing their thoughts, landlords set the foundation for effective feedback collection.

Step 2: Actively encourage feedback on a regular basis. This can be accomplished through various means, such as conducting surveys, providing suggestion boxes, or engaging in face-to-face conversations. The key is to convey that feedback is not only welcome but also highly valued.

Step 3: Pose specific questions that prompt thoughtful responses. Rather than asking broad questions like "How is your experience?", it is advisable to ask targeted questions that really dive into specific aspects of the tenancy, such as maintenance, communication, or amenities. This guarantees action-oriented feedback to drive improvement.

Step 4: Listen attentively and without judgment. Providing a non-judgmental and empathetic ear to tenants' feedback is crucial. This cultivates an atmosphere of trust and encourages tenants to openly express their thoughts and concerns.

Step 5: Take prompt and transparent action based on the feedback received. Once feedback has been obtained, it is essential to promptly address any concerns or suggestions. This showcases the landlord's commitment to continuous improvement, while also demonstrating that tenants' input is taken seriously.

Step 6: Communicate the actions taken in response to feedback. Tenants should be informed of the steps taken to address their feedback. This not only provides transparency but also demonstrates the direct impact that tenants' feedback has on their living experience.

By adhering to this step-by-step guide, landlords can effectively seek feedback from tenants and continually improve the overall rental experience. Seeking feedback has revolutionized the approach to being a landlord, enabling them to not only provide a well-maintained property but also create an environment that is truly pleasurable for tenants.

In conclusion, seeking feedback from tenants constitutes an essential aspect of ethical property management. It allows landlords to identify areas for improvement, address concerns, and enhance the overall rental experience. By establishing open communication, actively encouraging feedback, and taking prompt action, landlords can forge an environment that is both rewarding and enjoyable for tenants. Seeking feedback is not merely a means to improve property management, but also a way to cultivate trust and respect between landlords and tenants. Ultimately, the success of a landlord-tenant relationship thrives on this dynamic.

Professional Development and Education Opportunities

Industry conferences are significant events that bring together experts, professionals, and enthusiasts from the real estate and property management industry. Attending these conferences allows individuals to network with like-minded professionals, exchange ideas, and gain insights into current market trends and emerging opportunities. The workshops and seminars organized within these conferences provide an opportunity to learn from experienced industry leaders who share their expertise and practical advice.

I recall attending the National Landlord Conference last year, an experience that was truly transformative. The conference featured a wide range of sessions covering topics such as best practices in tenant screening, property maintenance, and legal updates. The keynote speakers were renowned experts in the field, and their presentations left a lasting impact on my understanding of the profession. I also had the chance to meet fellow landlords and property managers, and it was inspiring to hear about their experiences and achievements. The knowledge gained and the connections made at the conference have played a vital role in enhancing my management practices and expanding my professional network.

Apart from industry conferences, workshops offer focused and interactive learning opportunities. These sessions are usually conducted by subject matter experts who provide practical insights and guidance on specific areas of property management. Whether it involves learning about strategies for risk management or exploring innovative approaches to marketing rental properties, workshops offer valuable takeaways that can be directly applied to our businesses.

One workshop that particularly stood out was on effective communication with tenants. As landlords, clear and effective communication is crucial in maintaining positive relationships with tenants. This workshop emphasized the importance of active listening, respectful speaking, and prompt addressing of concerns. I acquired strategies for managing difficult conversations, resolving conflicts, and fostering a sense of community within rental properties. These skills have proven to be invaluable when dealing with tenant issues and have contributed to a more harmonious living environment for all parties involved.

While in-person conferences and workshops have their own merits, technological advancements have provided online resources for landlords seeking professional development. Websites, podcasts, webinars, and online courses have become accessible platforms that offer a wealth of information and education. The convenience of online resources allows individuals to learn at their own pace and on their preferred schedules, making it easier to incorporate education into busy lives.

One specific online resource that has been extremely beneficial on my journey as a landlord is a website called "The Ethical Landlord Academy." This platform offers a comprehensive range of courses and resources specifically tailored to ethical landlords. From modules on fair housing regulations to tutorials on sustainable property management practices, the academy covers all aspects of ethical property management. The interactive nature of the platform allows for engagement with other landlords and the opportunity to discuss and share ideas. The convenience and affordability of online resources such as these make them a valuable tool for continuous growth and improvement as a landlord.

It is important to note that engaging in professional development and education opportunities not only benefits individuals as landlords but also contributes to the improvement of the rental housing industry as a whole. By continually learning and staying informed about industry trends and best practices, landlords are better equipped to provide quality housing and foster positive relationships with their tenants.

Furthermore, ongoing education and professional development can also enhance the overall reputation of landlords and property managers. As ethical landlords, it is their responsibility to demonstrate a commitment to providing safe, affordable, and well-managed rental properties. By actively seeking out educational opportunities and staying informed about the latest industry standards, they showcase their dedication to continuous improvement and professionalism. This not only benefits their businesses but also contributes to the overall perception of landlords as responsible and trustworthy individuals.

To conclude, ongoing professional development and education opportunities offer invaluable benefits for ethical landlords. Industry conferences, workshops, and online resources provide avenues for networking, skill-building, and staying up-to-date with industry trends. By actively participating in these activities, landlords enhance their knowledge, improve their management practices, and contribute to the advancement of the rental housing industry. Investing in their own professional growth ultimately allows them to provide better quality housing and build stronger relationships with their tenants.

Collaborating With Other Ethical Landlords

Emphasizing the benefits of collaborating with other ethical landlords is of utmost importance. By forming alliances with fellow ethical landlords, we can combine our resources, knowledge, and expertise, ultimately enhancing our capacity to make a positive impact. Collectively, we have the opportunity to amplify our voices, influence policy changes, and empower one another to uphold the highest ethical standards in our rental endeavors.

Primarily, collaborating with other ethical landlords allows us to tap into a wealth of experience and knowledge. Each landlord possesses their own unique insights acquired through years of property management. Through the sharing of these experiences, we can learn from each other's successes and failures, ultimately advancing and refining our own practices. Engaging in conversations with other ethical landlords has led me to discover innovative strategies for minimizing vacancy rates, increasing tenant satisfaction, and ensuring the long-term sustainability of my properties. By leveraging the collective knowledge within the ethical landlord community, we become better equipped to overcome challenges and find practical solutions to the issues we encounter.

Additionally, working with other ethical landlords provides an avenue for networking and building valuable relationships. Collaborative efforts can materialize in various forms, such as establishing local landlord associations, attending industry conferences, or participating in online forums and communities. These platforms offer opportunities to engage with like-minded individuals and cultivate connections that extend beyond the confines of our immediate rental markets. Networking with other ethical landlords not only fosters a sense of camaraderie but also opens doors for potential partnerships, joint ventures, and even mentorship opportunities. Building these relationships allows us to tap into a broader network of resources, which can prove invaluable when navigating the various challenges that arise in the rental industry.

Sharing best practices is another crucial aspect of collaborating with other ethical landlords. Each landlord brings their own unique approach to property management, and by exchanging ideas, we can collectively raise our standards and enhance the quality of housing for tenants. For instance, through my own collaborative efforts, I have acquired insights into efficient systems for tenant screening, the implementation of sustainable practices, and conflict resolution. Sharing these best practices not only benefits our individual businesses but also helps set a higher bar for the entire rental industry.

Transparently sharing best practices is also indicative of our commitment to transparency, a fundamental tenet of ethical landlordship. By fostering a culture of knowledge-sharing, we can collectively identify and address key industry challenges, such as tenant discrimination, subpar housing conditions, or unfair rent pricing. Through collaboration, we can present a united front and advocate for systemic changes that safeguard both tenants' rights and the integrity of our industry.

To facilitate effective collaboration among ethical landlords, it is vital to establish platforms for knowledge-sharing and communication. Online forums, social media groups, and industry conferences serve as valuable spaces for ethical landlords to connect, exchange ideas, and work towards common goals. Local or regional landlord associations can also play a pivotal role in fostering collaboration at a grassroots level, enabling landlords to engage with their peers and collectively address local housing issues. Creating a network of ethical landlords who are committed to promoting fair and sustainable housing practices not only benefits us as individuals but also contributes to the wider social good by establishing a collective voice for positive change within the rental industry.

Collaborating with other ethical landlords affords an array of benefits. By harnessing the collective wisdom and experiences of like-minded individuals, we are better equipped to navigate challenges, enhance our practices, and advocate for transformative change within the rental industry. Through knowledge-sharing, networking, and joint efforts, we have the potential to create a more transparent, fair, and sustainable rental market. Together, let us endeavor to forge a future where ethical standards are not merely guiding principles but a shared reality for all landlords, tenants, and communities.

Inspiring Ethical Landlordship in Others

As a seasoned and accomplished ethical landlord, I firmly believe in the transformative power of mentorship and guidance in shaping the approach and responsibilities of aspiring landlords. Ethical landlordship, in my view, transcends the pursuit of mere profit, encompassing the creation of a safe and comfortable environment for tenants, a respect for their rights, and the overall positive contribution to society.

A valuable method for inspiring and mentoring aspiring ethical landlords lies in the sharing of personal experiences. Throughout my professional journey, I have encountered numerous challenges and obstacles that tested my commitment to ethical practices. By openly discussing these experiences and the lessons I have learned, I am able to provide invaluable insights and guidance to those entering the field.

For instance, there is a distinct memory etched in my mind when a tenant reported a serious plumbing issue in one of my rental properties. Instead of disregarding the problem or resorting to minimal and temporary fixes, I chose to make a comprehensive investment in overhauling the plumbing system. This decision not only ensured the welfare and satisfaction of the tenant but also maintained the integrity and long-term value of the property. By sharing this experience with aspiring ethical landlords, my aim is to instill in them the importance of prioritizing tenant well-being and making enduring investments that benefit all parties involved.

Alongside the sharing of personal experiences, providing guidance constitutes another integral aspect of inspiring ethical landlordship in others. It demands patience, understanding, and a commitment to fostering the growth of mentees. By establishing regular communication, I encourage open dialogue, inviting questions, advice-seeking, and discussions about any challenges they may face.

One notable piece of guidance I consistently emphasize is the critical significance of conducting thorough background checks on prospective tenants. It is essential to grasp their rental history, financial stability, and character to guarantee a harmonious and secure living environment for all tenants. I also stress the importance of clear and concise communication with tenants, promptly addressing any concerns or repairs, and cultivating a healthy professional relationship built on trust and mutual respect.

Moreover, advocating for ethical practices within the industry constitutes a potent tool for inspiring aspiring landlords. By actively engaging in industry organizations and collaborating with other professionals, I strive to advocate for the adoption of ethical practices and drive positive change in the field.

As part of this advocacy, I have taken the initiative to organize seminars and workshops that focus on ethical landlordship. These events bring together seasoned landlords, property managers, and aspiring landlords, providing a platform for knowledge exchange and discussions on ethical practices. By showcasing the benefits and success stories of ethical landlordship, my objective is to inspire genuine change and encourage others to embrace similar principles.

Additionally, I have actively lobbied for heightened regulations and policies that safeguard the rights of tenants and foster ethical behavior in the industry. Through engagement with local and national decision-makers, I advocate for legislation that ensures equitable treatment, promotes affordable housing, and discourages exploitative practices. My purpose in doing so is to foster an ethical environment that aspiring landlords can confidently enter and thrive in.

Inspiring ethical landlordship in others necessitates a comprehensive approach that encompasses personal experiences, guidance, and advocacy for ethical practices within the industry. By sharing personal stories, offering guidance, and advocating for positive change, mentors can shape the mindset and actions of aspiring ethical landlords. It is through this collective effort that we can cultivate a community of landlords who prioritize the well-being of their tenants, uphold ethical standards, and make a meaningful contribution to the societies they serve.

Chapter 9: The Path of the Ethical Landlord - A Comprehensive Guide

As we embark on the journey of ethical landlordship, it is crucial to recognize that our roles extend far beyond mere property management. We bear the profound responsibility of shaping communities, fostering trust, and upholding the highest standards of integrity. This final chapter serves as a comprehensive guide, encapsulating the core principles and practices that define the path of the ethical landlord.

Embodying the Ethical Mindset

The foundation of ethical landlordship lies in cultivating the right mindset – one that prioritizes the well-being of tenants, upholds transparency, and embraces a spirit of service. This mindset is characterized by unwavering commitment to the following principles:

1. Compassion and Empathy: Ethical landlords understand that their tenants are more than mere contractual obligations; they are individuals with unique circumstances, challenges, and aspirations. Cultivating empathy and compassion is essential to fostering positive relationships and creating a supportive environment that promotes tenant satisfaction and well-being.
2. Fairness and Non-Discrimination: Discrimination in any form, be it based on race, gender, religion, or any other protected characteristic, is antithetical to

ethical landlordship. Ethical landlords must uphold the principles of fair housing laws and treat all tenants with equal respect, dignity, and opportunity.

3. Transparency and Open Communication: Trust is the cornerstone of any successful landlord-tenant relationship, and transparency is the key to building that trust. Ethical landlords should strive for open and honest communication, providing clear and comprehensive information about policies, procedures, and expectations from the outset.

4. Continuous Learning and Improvement: The landscape of landlord-tenant laws, regulations, and best practices is ever-evolving. Ethical landlords must embrace a mindset of continuous learning, actively seeking out educational opportunities, staying abreast of industry changes, and continually refining their practices to better serve their tenants and communities.

5. Ethical Leadership and Advocacy: Ethical landlords are not mere observers; they are agents of positive change within their industry and communities. By embodying ethical principles and advocating for fair and equitable practices, they can inspire and influence others, fostering a culture of responsibility and integrity.

Implementing Ethical Practices

While cultivating the right mindset is essential, it is through the implementation of ethical practices that we truly fulfill our roles as ethical landlords. This subsection outlines key areas where ethical practices should be rigorously applied:

1. Tenant Screening and Selection:

○ Ensure fair and non-discriminatory screening processes

○ Clearly communicate criteria and requirements

○ Respect applicants' privacy and handle personal information with utmost care

2. Lease Agreements and Documentation:

○ Provide comprehensive and transparent lease agreements

○ Ensure compliance with all relevant laws and regulations

○ Explain terms and conditions in clear, accessible language

3. Property Maintenance and Repairs:

○ Maintain properties to the highest safety and habitability standards

○ Respond promptly to repair requests and address issues in a timely manner

○ Prioritize sustainability and energy-efficient practices

4. Tenant Communication and Conflict Resolution:

○ Foster open and respectful communication channels

○ Actively seek tenant feedback and address concerns promptly

○ Establish fair and impartial conflict resolution processes

5. Rent Increases and Terminations:

○ Provide ample notice and justification for any rent increases

○ Ensure compliance with all applicable laws and regulations

○ Handle terminations with empathy and respect for tenants' rights

6. Community Engagement and Social Responsibility:

○ Promote a sense of community among tenants

○ Engage in charitable initiatives and support local causes

○ Prioritize sustainable and environmentally responsible practices

Navigating Ethical Challenges

Despite our best efforts, ethical landlords may encounter complex situations that test their principles and values. This subsection aims to provide guidance on navigating some of the most challenging ethical dilemmas:

1. Balancing Business Interests and Tenant Well-being:

○ Recognize that short-term financial gains should never compromise tenant well-being or ethical standards

○ Seek innovative solutions that align business objectives with ethical practices

○ Foster open dialogues with tenants to find mutually beneficial resolutions

2. Addressing Disruptive or Problematic Tenants:

○ Establish clear policies and procedures for addressing tenant misconduct

○ Prioritize open communication and provide opportunities for corrective action

○ Ensure due process and respect for tenants' rights, even in challenging situations

3. Navigating Legal and Regulatory Complexities:

○ Stay informed about changes in landlord-tenant laws and regulations

○ Seek guidance from legal professionals when needed

○ Advocate for fair and equitable policies within the industry

4. Ethical Dilemmas in Crisis Situations:

○ Develop contingency plans for emergencies and crisis scenarios

○ Prioritize the safety and well-being of tenants above all else

○ Maintain transparency and open communication during challenging times

5. Confronting Personal Biases and Ethical Blind Spots:

○ Engage in self-reflection and actively seek feedback

○ Embrace diversity and strive for cultural competence

○ Seek out mentors and advisors who can offer objective perspectives

As ethical landlords, we must navigate these challenges with unwavering commitment to our principles, while also recognizing the complexities and nuances of each situation. By remaining steadfast in our pursuit of ethical practices, we can overcome obstacles and serve as beacons of integrity within our industry and communities.

The path of the ethical landlord is a journey of unwavering commitment, continuous growth, and unwavering dedication to upholding the highest standards of integrity. By embodying the ethical mindset, implementing ethical practices, and navigating challenges with wisdom and compassion, we can transform the rental industry into one that prioritizes the well-being of tenants, fosters trust, and contributes to the betterment of our communities.

As we conclude this comprehensive guide, let us embrace the words of esteemed philosopher John Rawls: "Justice is the first virtue of social institutions, as truth is of systems of thought." May these words serve as a guiding light, reminding us that our roles as ethical landlords extend far beyond mere business transactions; we are stewards of justice, champions of fairness, and architects of a more equitable society.

Embark on this journey with conviction, courage, and an unwavering commitment to ethical principles. For it is through our collective efforts that we can create a future where ethical landlordship is not merely an aspiration but a celebrated reality.

Addendum: Resources for Ethical Landlords

Being an ethical landlord requires ongoing education, access to reliable resources, and a commitment to continuous improvement. This addendum provides a curated list of links, books, and other resources to support landlords in upholding ethical practices and staying informed about the latest developments in the industry.

Online Resources and Links:

1. U.S. Department of Housing and Urban Development (HUD) - Fair Housing:https://www.hud.gov/program_offices/fair_housing_equal_opp

○ Comprehensive information on fair housing laws, rights, and responsibilities for landlords.

2. Landlord-Tenant Laws by State:https://www.nolo.com/legal-encyclopedia/free-books/landlord-book/chapter1-1.html

○ A comprehensive guide to landlord-tenant laws across different states, provided by Nolo.

3. National Apartment Association (NAA) - Industry Resources:https://www.naahq.org/resources

○ Valuable resources, including webinars, publications, and best practices for property management.

4. National Association of Residential Property Managers (NARPM):https://www.narpm.org/

○ Professional organization for residential property managers, offering education, certifications, and industry insights.

5. Energy Star for Landlords and Property Managers:https://www.energystar.gov/buildings/owners_and_managers

○ Resources and guidance on implementing energy-efficient practices in rental properties.

6. EPA Healthy Indoor Air for Landlords:https://www.epa.gov/indoor-air-quality-iaq/healthy-indoor-air-landlords

○ Information and resources on maintaining healthy indoor air quality in rental properties.

7. HUD Fair Housing Accessibility Requirements:https://www.hud.gov/program_offices/fair_housing_equal_opp/disabilities/accessibilityR

o Guidelines and requirements for ensuring accessibility in rental properties for people with disabilities.

Recommended Books:

1. "Landlording on Auto-Pilot" by Mike Butler

o A practical guide to efficient and ethical property management, covering tenant screening, maintenance, and more.

2. "The Book on Managing Rental Properties" by Brandon Turner and Heather Turner

o A comprehensive resource on managing rental properties, including ethical practices and legal considerations.

Online Courses and Certifications:

1. National Apartment Association Education Institute (NAAEI):https://www.naahq.org/education-careers/naa-education-institute

o Offers various courses, certifications, and training programs for property managers and landlords.

2. National Center for Housing Management (NCHM):https://www.nchm.org/

○ Provides training and certifications for housing managers, including courses on fair housing, ethics, and legal compliance.

3. Coursera:https://www.coursera.org/

○ Online learning platform offering courses on property management, real estate, and related topics from universities and industry experts.

4. edX:https://www.edx.org/

○ Another online learning platform with courses on real estate, property management, and sustainable practices.

Local Resources:

1. State and local housing authorities

○ Many states and municipalities have housing authorities that provide resources, guidelines, and training for landlords.

2. Housing associations and organizations

○ Local housing associations and organizations often offer workshops, seminars, and networking opportunities for landlords.

3. Community colleges and universities

○ Many community colleges and universities offer continuing education courses or certificate programs related to property management and landlord responsibilities.

By utilizing these resources, links, and recommended books, landlords can stay informed about ethical practices, legal requirements, and industry best practices. Continuous learning and access to reliable information are essential for maintaining high standards and providing a positive experience for tenants while upholding ethical principles.

Don't miss out!

Visit the website below and you can sign up to receive emails whenever Jack Donahue publishes a new book. There's no charge and no obligation.

https://books2read.com/r/B-A-WCSZ-NSNHD

BOOKS 2 READ

Connecting independent readers to independent writers.

Did you love *The Complete Ethical Landlord*? Then you should read *Apartment Hunting For Devil Worshippers*[1] by Jack Donahue!

[2]

In the bustling world of modern apartment living, creating a harmonious balance between physical space and spiritual practice can be a complex task, especially for the devout Devil Worshipper. Apartment Hunting For Devil Worshippers is a comprehensive resource designed to guide you through this unique journey.

The book covers a wide range of topics, from practical considerations like finding and viewing potential apartments

---

1. https://books2read.com/u/brBZke

2. https://books2read.com/u/brBZke

and understanding landlord-tenant laws, to spiritual matters such as setting up your Small Space, Sacred Place, and arranging your altar. We delve into acoustic considerations for maintaining a peaceful inner sanctuary amidst the noise of the city, and provide strategies for handling sensitive practices, such as Satanic rituals.

Throughout the guide, we interweave practical advice with spiritual insights to not just enhance your daily life but to deepen your understanding and practice of devil worship. Whether you're an experienced practitioner on the Left Hand Path, or you're new to the Devil worshippers lifestyle, Apartment Hunting For Devil Worshippers provides a wealth of information tailored to your needs.

Join us on this journey towards achieving religious freedom within the confines of apartment living, and learn to create a home that truly resonates with your beliefs, nourishes your spirit, and empowers your devil worship. This is your guide to occult living, a path to merging the mundane and the mystical in your daily life.

Also by Jack Donahue

Apartment Hunting For Devil Worshippers
Puzzling Patriarchy: Understanding Adult Words for Little Thinkers
I Gave Up Hope And Died... And It Worked!
The Conservative Agenda
Empowering Local Leadership
The Complete Ethical Landlord